WHAT DO AMERICAN SCHOOLS NEED?
A HANDBOOK FOR PARENTS, STUDENTS, EDUCATORS AND COMMUNITY

WHAT DO AMERICAN SCHOOLS NEED?
A HANDBOOK FOR PARENTS, STUDENTS, EDUCATORS AND COMMUNITY

ANNE G. GARRETT

Kroshka Books
Commack, New York

Editorial Production:	Susan Boriotti
Office Manager:	Annette Hellinger
Graphics:	Frank Grucci and John T'Lustachowski
Information Editor:	Tatiana Shohov
Book Production:	Donna Dennis, Patrick Davin, Christine Mathosian and Tammy Sauter
Circulation:	Maryanne Schmidt
Marketing/Sales:	Cathy DeGregory

Library of Congress Cataloging-in-Publication Data

Garrett, Anne G..

What do American Schools Need? A Handbook for Parents, Students, Educators and Community / by Anne G. Garrett.

p.   cm.

ISBN 1-56072-583-4

1. Public Schools--United States. 2. Education Aids and Policies--United States. 3. Moral education--United States 4. Educational change--United States I. Title.

1998   98-43134
                                                                                                                    CIP

Copyright © 1999 by Anne G. Garrett
Kroshka Books, a division of
Nova Science Publishers, Inc.
6080 Jericho Turnpike, Suite 207
Commack, New York 11725
Tele. 516-499-3103   Fax 516-499-3146
e-mail: Novascience@earthlink.net
e-mail: Novascil@aol.com
Web Site: http://www.nexusworld.com/nova

Printed in the United States of America

To Gary, the love of my life. Thank you for your support throughout my career.

CONTENTS

ABOUT THE AUTHOR

Anne Garrett is the co-author of seven previous books, *Five Minute Fillers, Listening Skills, Teach Children to Speak, Teach Children to Listen, Geography Activities Book, Social Studies Activities Book, and Vocational Educational Activities Book.* An educator for over twenty years who specializes in curriculum and instructional, she has worked in the public schools. Her wide range of experiences include teacher, lead teacher, assistant principal, principal, supervisor and director. Currently she is an associate superintendent in North Carolina. Her numerous educational degrees include elementary, middle grades, reading, mathematics, supervision, administration, superintendent, and curriculum specialist. Her doctorate degree was obtained from the University of North Carolina at Greensboro. Garrett lives with her husband Gary in Clyde, North Carolina. Her philosophy, includes adaptation from Plato, The Republic, "The direction in which education starts a child will determine his or her future." Also, "The solution of adult problems tomorrow depends in large measure upon the way our children grow up today. There is no greater insight into the future than recognizing when we save our children, we save ourselves" (Margaret Mead).

WHAT DO AMERICAN SCHOOLS NEED?

Taxpayers are confused and are not supporting the public schools as they have in years past. For several years now, the public has sent a clear message that what it is most concerned about in public education is the perceived lack of student safety and student discipline and the poor attention given by teachers to the basic academic subjects. Talk of private and charter schools and the voucher system are real possibilities and taxpayers are ready for a change. What has happened to lower the trust of public schools and what can we do? WHAT DO AMERICAN SCHOOLS NEED? is an attempt to place public education as the new paradigm and verify how it will be a process that encourages continual progress through the improvement and expansion in the schools. Schools simply cannot function as they have in the past or they will be out of business; changes in our educational system must be made and soon. The last thing we need is another pilot project or a novel approach that promises to prepare our children for the 21st century. What we really need is to educate our parents, prepare our children and build character. The lives of children who enroll in school today will span a new century. The nation's prospects for the future will be dangerously diminished if the coming generation cannot be helped to reach their potential. These premises do not need another curriculum guide or millions of dollars spent. We have the resources at our fingertips that will enable us to educate our future leaders.

The African proverb, it takes a whole village to raise a single child is becoming very popular especially with the release of IT TAKES A VILLAGE, First Lady Hillary Clinton. Creating quality American schools for our children indeed involves all stakeholders; schools cannot stand alone. The following questions are the premises for writing WHAT DO AMERICAN SCHOOLS NEED? How do you get all stakeholders involved? What's the correlation between quality and school? How do you relate the curriculum of the classroom to the ethical and moral lives of children? Finally, educators alone cannot make our schools better and prepare children for the workplace.

        Anne G. Garrett

CHAPTER ONE

WHO ARE OUR CUSTOMERS?
HOW DO WE CREATE A SHARED
VISION?

Unless all students come to school each day ready to learn - meaning they are healthy, rested, nourished, and attentive - schools will be marginally effective. In particular, schools alone cannot overcome the desperate conditions of poverty-stricken students. In a quality education system, collaboration between schools, families, governments, and social agencies is paramount (American Association of School Administrators, 1992, p. 14).

The 1995 Phi Delta Kappa/Gallup of the Public's Attitudes Toward the Public Schools, features the exploration of several significant national educational issues. People continue to rate the schools in their communities much higher than they rate the nation's schools. Approximately 65% of public school parents assigned an A or to the school their oldest child attends. Lack of discipline and financial support were viewed as the major problems facing the schools. People viewed lack of parent control and the breakdown of family life as major causes of the increase in school violence. There continues to be strong public support for the introduction of higher academic standards in the public schools. The desire for public school prayer continues to be strong. Parents indicated considerable involvement with the schools. Over the years the ratings for local schools have been stationary and eighty-nine percent indicated they would be willing to sign a contract which would specify everyone's responsibilities - the school's, the child's and the parent's. If this poll is accurate then why are schools being criticized by the public? PHI DELTA KAPPAN's editor, Pauline B. Gough, responded to the Gallup poll by saying the respondents to the annual survey lacked direct knowledge of the schools. "Their responses reflect information culled from the mass media or from other secondhand sources - much of it slanted and unflattering, if not actually false" (1995, p. 2). She further stated that regardless of how true the polls were the respondents' views of the schools are very influential and will affect everything from education legislation and funding to professional development and staff morale. The Graustein Memorial Fund and the Public Agenda Foundation conducted a survey to determine why the citizens in Connecticut failed to support reform. The result was those surveyed felt the schools were headed in the wrong direction. Their view was that educators and the schools had broken the contract with the public. They identified four areas in which they thought the schools were going wrong. The areas included:

Safety. Only 28% thought schools were doing a good job in this area. Keeping schools free of drugs, crime and gangs got top priority (81%).

Parents. Eighty two percent surveyed felt parents were not doing their job by fulfilling their responsibilities toward education and toward their own children.

Basics. Being able to speak and write English clearly before graduation was important to 94%. Yet 58% thought the schools were not doing a good job of teaching the basics.

Discipline and respect for authority. There was a very strong feeling that schools were not stressing discipline or teaching good working habits.

"The bottom line is the public's thinking that these things can be fixed without additional money. The public also felt that the big boost the state gave to teacher salaries in the 1980's hadn't produced any visible payoff" (Pipho, p. 582).

Is a school reform on the agenda?

People don't understand why reforms are necessary and should be considered better because people have not been impressed with reforms that have previously taken place. Criticism of the public schools increased after World War II and has never receded. The media gives inordinate amounts of attention to critics and much less to those who are advocates of the system. Thus, the baby boomers and their children have always heard the negative aspect of education.

Frank Smith (April, 1995) states we should quit worrying about the problems of education, "Declare it a disaster, and let teachers and students get on with their lives. The trouble with the endless concern over problems in education is that many well-meaning but often misguided, meddlesome people believe solutions must exist." He further states we should change the way we talk about schools by talking less, teaching more and doing more" (p. 585).

Our demographics have changed dramatically. One of two marriages now end in divorce and fifty-five percent of the households are headed by a single mother. More than half of all children under eighteen have a mother who works outside the home, often out of economic necessity. Every year one family out of five moves. Have these statistics affected our children?

In a lot of families, the school is the only stabilizing force in their environment. Children don't come in neat little packages to school ready to learn; they carry excess baggage with them such as hunger and lack of parental support.

Schools can improve children's conduct while they are in school but the likelihood of it lasting is decreased if parents do not follow up at home. This reason alone should be significant enough to bring parents and community working together with the schools for a common cause. Working together creates real power to raise up moral human beings in both character development and the academics. "The school system can't make up for the family failure. The total education of our children is a cooperative effort requiring community solidarity. Apathetic parents who foster a permissive home atmosphere create a problem for everyone" (Thomas Lickona, 1991).

Deborah Meier, in her book, THE POWER OF THEIR IDEAS: LESSONS FOR AMERICA FROM A SMALL SCHOOL IN HARLEM (1995), states that good schools are havens for intelligent, caring adults who respect each other and the children they care for. Success is not necessarily measured by curriculum and test scores but by creating a caring environment and stable place for our children. Maybe it's the gray area between school and family that we are seeking hope.

"Researchers often jump to hasty conclusions, overgeneralizing from far too little data....but I also know the power of a good school and of caring and demanding teachers" (Barr, 1996, p. 382). The long term success of schools and educating children depends on forces outside the schools - families and communities joining schools in a common effort to meet the needs of children and foster healthy development.

Who is involved in educating children? Our customers who are students, teachers, principals, custodians, bus-drivers, parents, community - anyone who has a vested interest in education.

Building a true community of learning is the first and most essential ingredient of an effective school (Boyer, 1995). It's impossible to achieve excellence in the schools where goals are unrecognizable and missions are unclear, where teachers and students cannot communicate and where the parents and community are uninvolved in educating the children. Building good relationships with our customers does not just happen - it takes time, energy and effort.

A customer is anyone that uses the product or is involved in producing the product. When people are providing goods, information or services to the organization or structure; these individuals are our customers. Each person in the school setting - student, certified and non-certified personnel, parents and community - are our customers. For schools, some customers are external such as community members without school age children or businesses and industries. Customers who are internal are those who provide products and services directly to the school. The schools' most important customers may be the staff, parents and children attending or directly involved in the school.

Central office administrators, site principals, and teachers are customers and suppliers of each other. Principals may supply teachers with the legal parameters of a school budget, management of curriculum and codes of conduct. Teachers may supply principals with information about student needs, achievement, curriculum recommendations and methodologies of instruction.

Between teachers and students there should exist a common knowledge of supplier and satisfying the customer's needs. Teachers provide the service of facilitating and coaching the instructional program and assessing the end product. Students are the reason for the existence of schools and they provide the teacher with feedback on instructional progress.

The American Association of School Administrators (1992) recommend the following in transforming a school system to a customer/supplier perspective:

1. The entire school system becomes a service system at every level and involves all people in the system.
2. The system will gain power from a shared mission or vision. The service orientation should not exist to merely please or impress the customer.
3. In a customer/supplier relationship, every person is a winner because each individual is working for the success of the organization.
4. Competition between the customer and supplier is not needed nor desirable.

The customer/supplier perspective focuses on the interdependence and reciprocity of all who are involved in the lives of children.

Maintaining a commitment to systematic fundamental change in school districts requires establishing new partnerships among all of a community's services and agencies that influence the healthy development of children and learning.

The problem confronting American schools are substantial; the resources available to them are in most instances severely limited; the stakes are high, and it is by no means preordained that all will go well for many of them in the end.

American schools are in real trouble. The problems of schools and taxpayers distrust and lack of confidence in the public schools is overwhelming. It is possible that the entire national school system may be going out of business. We will continue to have schools but choices will be available to all in the form of charter schools, private schooling with a nice tax deduction, vouchers and home-schooling, will rule the educational process. The relationship between these school offerings and families, communities, and states could be quite different from what we now know.

)

For public education to survive, substantial faith and confidence must be reinstated at the school level. Demographics have changed - the proportion of citizens not directly involved in the schools has increased. The primary clients - parents with school age children are a minority.

American has not outgrown its need for schools. If schools ceased to exist tomorrow - it would be necessary for someone to reinvent them. But the public school cannot go on with business as usual. A reconstruction has to take place and in the near future. Again, we must call upon our customers for advice, consultation and implementation.

The schools we need are not necessarily the schools we have today. Society has tended to bash the schools rather than seek alternatives. Criticism links back to the 1950's when the focus was children not being able to read - the focus was not necessarily on the school administrators and those institutions that train teachers. In the 1960's attack was underway stating students were not being renewed - facts and not hypotheses were being taught. The 1970's criticism focused on the school itself - not the staff. The 1980's brought criticism with academics – our schools were not teaching what our children needed to know and what they were being tested on. This phase of academic criticism continued in the 1990's. The 1990's also fell under attack to overall dissatisfaction with the operations of the schools, academics, school climate, violence, not teaching to meet individual needs, lack of students having fun and learning at the same time, and standards declining.

Parents and community members want a comprehensive education for children. Parents also want the major part of education to be done in the schools. For most parents life is very demanding. Over seventy percent of the mothers have entered the workforce. There's little time for recreation with children, let alone time to provide formal education. Schools today do not merely educate but they are caregivers as well.

Schools need to provide programs that respond to the unique needs of elementary, middle and high schools families and students. In addition to going through physiological changes in children, parents must also deal with changes that are taking place within the schools.

Educating children is a unique challenge to families, schools and districts as they strive to create strong partnerships to promote quality education. These partnerships should go beyond information exchange to creating school change and the creation of relationships that contribute to student success. Each partnership will take planing and a synergist leader and parents and community must support the changes in teaching that are at the heart of student success.

How can we provide quality schools with support and satisfy our customers' needs?

Schools need to commit to genuine parent partnerships. We often give lip service to having an open door policy. The real door must open with a genuine desire and with our attitude. As educators, how involved do we want parents or do we want them involved? If we sincerely want parents involved in the educational process then we must walk our talk. We must believe that parents are still the child's first and most important teacher and that family is the most important institution in our society. It is our job to help parents know how to parent and let them know they know how to parent. Many parents are isolated and if we respect and trust them as equals they should respond. By strong school leadership, we can network parents and help them provide support for their children. We need a sincere commitment. Schools must first find ways to work successfully with parents. Few schools have achieved this goal and not for a long term. The other suppliers - community, legislatures, taxpayers, teacher preparation institutions - also must play their part. We need to all be involved in the new paradigm of education. The new paradigm is redesigning the system in which we meet our customers' needs. The focus is on the quality of the service we are providing not the pyramid of command. This new paradigm is focused on continuous improvement and customer satisfaction. Typically, in education we've tried something three years and then moved to something else - we haven't stayed with anything long enough to determine if it works or doesn't. We find ourselves facing same buzz words and teaching methodologies as we did twenty years ago - simply because they have gone the 380 degrees and are now back with us. We've thrown money at problems rather than looking at the management of the system.

The first step in this much needed educational reform and new paradigm is to get a buy in from our customers.

We need to become educated on how the world has changed and share this knowledge with our customers. As educators it is our job to provide an education for our children we have, not the children we used to have, or those we dream about. When educators investigate, we will find that our children have never been in greater need of the affective domain or Maslow's Hierarchy of Needs. All cognitive learning begins in the affective domain. Providing support and caring for students could very well be the most important factor in motivating higher thinking skills. The basic characteristics of any system are a set of interacting forces working for agreed upon purposes. W. Edward Deming said, "Without an aim or purpose, there is no system." Each school system must identify the system's aim or purpose. There is no right aim or purpose, it's what fits the system and satisfies the customer that's right. Some schools have selected the following aims or purposes:

- Every child a winner.
- To develop lifelong learners.
- All children reading on grade level by third grade.
- To provide a comprehensive, challenging, integrated, and sequential curriculum which insures successful learning experiences for all students
- To provide a technology rich environment for students, school personnel, and community members
- To increase effective communications and encourage community involvement for the benefit of all students.
- To provide student services so that all students have an optimum opportunity for social, emotional and academic growth
- To provide all students with facilities conducive to learning.
- To develop students who enjoy learning
- To make learning relevant to real-life situations
- To enable parents to become effective education partners
- To reinforce traditional values and positive character that originate and are fostered at home.
- To raise expectations for our children to maintain the status of our schools.
- To provide ever-increasing benefits for everyone in the community.

Developing a shared vision with the customers and the schools should be viewed as a community. The school's mission should be a place where everyone comes together to promote learning.

Boyer (1995) recommends a school as being purposeful, with a clear mission and goals. A shared mission, especially one that is intrinsic, uplifts people and their dreams. Work becomes part of pursuing a larger purpose.

How do you obtain a mission statement with goals?

In creating a shared mission statement and goals it should be one that each participant can understand and support; all customers should buy into it. Individuals in the school system need to know how they relate to the purpose, how their work contributes to the larger picture; the global effect. The school system's mission should benefit everyone in the larger community. "The clarity and desirability of the school system's aim gets everyone working together cooperatively to achieve that aim" (American Association of School Administrators, p. 10).

W. Edwards Deming's (1982) first point for quality schools is "Create a constancy of purpose for the improvement of product and service." Adopt a new philosophy - put quality first - this requires clear definitions. He emphasized design, test, and refine. We are at the designing stage at this point. Quality is not the problem but quality is the solution to the problem. Without a clearly defined mission, where will you know where you're headed? What direction will you take? How will you know when you've gotten there. Constancy is the key word because it requires you to have a firmly developed overview of the wants and needs of the school. This normally involves both long and short range planning. All customers need to be involved. Unless the faculty, parents, students and community have a clearly defined mission and a plan to implement it the classroom will be havoc and good student learning will never take place.

Developing a mission statement with clearly defined goals is not an easy task for the classroom, school or system. Let's begin on a smaller level - the classroom. A starting point would be for the teacher to develop a mission statement. For example a seventh grade science teacher might state:

To facilitate students' learning about principles of earth, life and physical science by seeking new knowledge and students understanding the need to reach beyond self to comprehend and control his or her world.

After this has been developed reflect on it. How can it be improved? Does it convey what really needs to be taught? Is it based on proven principles? Mission statements should be a result of your beliefs about students and education. Now, set your goals both short and long range. For example: The following will be facilitated:

Nature of Science	Process Skills
Manipulative Skills	Attitudes Toward Science
Current Topics	Systems and Diversity
Energy Concepts	

Students will show eighty-five percent mastery of each category. A variety of assessment tools will be used and they include: student portfolio, journal writing, group projects and written/teacher assessments.

A kindergarten teacher wanted to develop a mission statement in her classroom. She chose to discuss the helper chart and let each child choose a job for the day (distribute crayons, hand out paper, close the door, be first in line). Next they discussed how everyone had a different idea about what they wanted to do. A book was read to them in which the theme was helping hands and manners. They discussed the book and how it was important in their classroom. The teacher discussed a mission and gave several examples. For example, our mission is to make children learn and want to come to school each day. Children then shared why they wanted to come to school each day. The mission was developed from the students' input and the result was:

Our mission is to come to school each day so we can make new friends, and do things for ourselves. We will be good listeners, follow school rules, be honest and use good manners. We will do our best work and learn new skills that will help us all of our life.

Goals should be measurable and they should extend the learner. They should be aligned with the building and district goals.

Share these goals with your students. Communicate clearly and effectively. If students feel the goals are unrealistic or not challenging enough - allow them to discuss the issues. If students are not comfortable doing this - you might consider allowing them to work in small groups and discuss the issues. Appoint a recorder and a reporter. However, be sure to bring the entire group back together so reporters can share. This doesn't need to turn into a grip session where nothing is accomplished except complaining. Share the county or the state's Standard Course of Study so students will be familiar with the requirements.

Share the mission statement and goals with parents and community. A lot of schools conduct Open House or designated P.T.A./P.T.O. nights where time is allocated for curriculum sharing and discussing. The mission statement and goals need to be in writing so parents can take them home and reflect. Those parents not in attendance will need a copy. Consider calling those parents (Phonemaster - which is a computerized telecommunications, can do this for you). Ask parents to come visit during your planning time or before or after school. Still - you haven't reached one hundred percent of your parents - mail them this important information. When explaining the mission and goals to the parents, ask for input.

During parent orientation night (P.T.A., Open House), share the following with your parents:

Parent Orientation Night
Class: Mrs. Jones' Fourth Grade
Our Mission Statement
As your child's teacher I expect:

1. Students to come to school each day prepared to learn.
2. Parents to communicate with me.
3. Students to accept responsibility for their work and actions.
4. Parents to listen to children read and assist with assignments.

Your child expects:

1. The teacher to help them learn.
2. Teacher and parents to teach responsibility and how to be good citizens.
3. Parents to get them to school on time with the things they need.
4. Parents to help with assignments

As a parent I expect:

1. My child to listen and behave in class.
2. To do all of her work
3. To be nice and respectful to other children and to the teacher
4. The teacher to tell me if there's a problem and help me.

Display the mission statement and goals in your classroom, or hallway - make it highly visible. All correspondents to parents should have this information on it - this will allow for everyone to become familiar with the mission and goals. Also, provide students and parents with copies of the district's mission and goals.

Develop a means of keeping track of goals, how they are accomplished and at what rate. This could be done using a simple chart and posting it in the classroom.

Remember the teacher is the coach and facilitator of learning and their role is to focus on the mission and goals while assisting all students to achieve them.

Encourage parents and community to become involved in the learning process. State your expectations very clearly to them. Maintain a constancy of purpose by making the written mission statement and goals evident in the classroom. This also assists in aligning all activities in the classroom towards learning for a lifetime and success for tomorrow.

To be effective, school systems must create and endorse a mission statement and goals which are supported by all customers. If you enter a school, how many people can tell you the system's mission statement and goals? While talking to parents, how many of them can give you this information correctly? What about students, do they know the system's mission statement and goals? How can one fit into an organization when one has not been properly educated and they don't have or know the purpose?

There should be meetings to inform the staff, students, parents and community about the system's mission and the goals.

If the system does not have a clearly defined mission and goals they are usually fragmented and headed in no particular direction. How can you fit into an organization if the organization doesn't know the course it's headed and the direction to get there?

A shared mission especially one with goals uplifts peoples' spirits and aspiration because they want to know the direction they are taking or the road most traveled. Work then becomes part of pursuing a larger purpose and knowing how you fit into the "big picture." The mission can also be embodied in the style, climate and attitude of the organization. Missions are exciting and uplifting. They can create the spark and lift a mundane organization. A shared mission changes peoples' relationships with the school and system. A shared mission is the first step in allowing people to build interpersonal relationships - because they have a common bond. Schools must be a communicative, purposeful place where people are encouraged to speak and listen to each other. Adopt a customer focus to exceed their expectations. The mission statement and goals need to be developed with a plan as the end result and make decisions based on the identified needs. Establish a process for quality control - periodic assessment processes to insure customer satisfaction and achievement levels. Determine who your customers are, what they want, when do they need it and what is their satisfaction level. Develop a framework between schools and customers by involving customers in all aspects of quality.

We are always rushing into things and trying to fix them with good advice. We often fail to take the time to diagnose and really understand the problem because we are constantly looking for that "quick fix." The single most important habit of Covey's is to "Seek first to understand." Most people do not listen with the intent to understand; they listen with the intent to reply. "They're either speaking or preparing to speak. They're filtering through their own paradigms, reading their own autobiography into other people's lives" (p. 239). They project their own thoughts and experiences into other people's behavior. We owe it to our customers to make sure they are listening and getting the needed information before pre-judged opinions are formed. This can be accomplished by developing an atmosphere of trust between all customers.

Empathic listening is a key in seeking to understand first. It allows you to get accurate data to work with instead of merely projecting your thoughts and behaviors. You have turned the paradigm - you are listening to understand and you're focused on receiving the communication.

The new Carnegie Report recommends that building a true community of learning is the first and most element of an effective school. In their study, they concluded that it was virtually impossible to achieve educational excellence in schools where the mission was unclear, where teachers and students failed to communicate with each other, and where parents were uninvolved in the education of their children. "Community is, without question, the glue that holds an effective school together" (Boyer, p. 2).

Community doesn't just happen over night. Boyer defines community as "Something far more than a sentimental slogan or a message to be sent home to parents at the beginning of the year. What we are talking about is the culture of the school, the way people relate to one another, their attitudes and values" (Boyer, p. 2, 1995). To achieve community a school must be purposeful, with a clear mission, a communicative place, where people speak and listen, a place where everyone is treated fairly, a disciplined place where a code of conduct has been established, a caring place, where students feel secure. and a place where success is celebrated.

The schools must begin today to broaden the role of the school in relation to the community. There is a need for schools to function as community centers for students and their families. The rising number of families with single parents or two working parents adds validity to the need for schools to provide support and community. Educators who want families to participate in their child's education must give the school a role in helping to enrich family life. We need to bond with our community and form a partnership. Most communities are very supportive of the schools when it comes to physiological needs. The community churches and organizations continue to provide clothing, school supplies and medication to school children. But, the need is much great than Maslow's physiological hierarchy. We need more active involvement in which the community can act as resources and assist children with the educational process. There is always a demand for quality volunteers in the schools. It doesn't take much effort to listen to a child read daily but it does take commitment. We need to use our community for resources other than financially.

To encourage parents' involvement in their children education, Motorola, Inc. invites school officials and P.T.A. representatives to talk to parents in the work place, gives parents time off from work to attend parent-teacher conferences, and regularly distributes information to employees on improving students' academic performance. To encourage innovative teaching, Motorola, Pratt and Whitney, Florida Power and Light, and IBM, sponsor a four-day institute on creative math and science instruction for middle school teachers conducted by the Center for Advanced Teaching Techniques. To help improve students' basic communication skills, NCNB provides two hours of release time per week for employees who want to volunteer in the schools. These are all relevant examples of business and industry and their willingness to become partners with educational systems.

Several states are getting parents more involved in the schools and forming partnerships in the best interest of children. States (North Carolina, South Carolina and Georgia), have developed an addendum to their School Improvement Plans. Schools are actually asked to keep data on parent involvement. The goals/indicators for parent involvement include: parents as teachers, parents as learners, parents as decision-makers, and parents as supporters/advocators. Baseline data is established and a status is reported annually.

Building community support is becoming a big responsibility for the schools. Many administrators have asked school sites to have advisory councils and to give advice and direction for school improvement. Formation of a council can be locally mandated or at the request of a site administrator. A major reason for establishing a council would be to build broad-based accountability for decisions affecting the school, creating a stronger focus on a results-oriented improvement agenda and enhancing a sense of community among all elements of the school population.

A typical council would include eight to ten people and would consist of parents, teachers, students, support staff and community leaders. Involving the P.T.A. is a good beginning place for the selection of parent members. Most council members serve a two year term with staggered entrances. Results of the council meetings can be distributed through newsletters and oral reports. The council activities and involvement varies from site to site. Some deal directly with managing school assemblies, designing field day events, and fund-raising. Most councils assist with school improvement in which they assist with surveys and collecting data. One council's focus was to develop an outdoor physical facility. The group was totally responsible for developing a time line, reporting to the community and implementing a plan. The final result was a $110,000 project which included new playground equipment for intermediate grades, a 400 meter, six lane track, junior and senior soccer fields, additional parking places, sidewalk with rock wall, basketball goals and a walking lane. This example illustrates the commitment of a council to a given project.

"Community has to do with the deep structure fabric of interpersonal relations. Soundly woven, this fabric permits a shared frame of reference and supports mutual expectations" (Rossi and Stringfield, p. 74). Ten elements have been identified that characterize adult, student, and adult/student relations in the schools that are true communities:

- Shared vision
- Sense of purpose
- Shared values
- Incorporation of diversity
- Communication
- Participation
- Caring
- Trust
- Teamwork
- Respect and recognition (Rosi and Stringfield)

Schools that continually strengthen these elements are building the necessary foundation for developing community schools of excellence.

Communication and school involvement are correlated. Open door policies and open forums are important tools for the communication process. The customer must be comfortable in speaking and listening to others involved in this process. P.T.A. Executive Boards must have both parents and school staff members serving to be effective, this provides experiences in decision making both in learning about the school situation and instructional approaches. Executive members often can recommend new strategies or modifications in current practice; this is a good place for the site council to become involved.

Caring, trust and good teamwork characterize an effective communication process and active participation by all parties at the school site. Many school sites have established a family atmosphere to engender feelings of trust in students and colleagues. This is especially evident with the middle school concept in which advisee/advisor scheduling is permitted. Caring, trust and teamwork often is the result of sharing the challenges posed by new programs, students with special needs, teachers in specialty areas, or school and community problems.

The initial criticism in the schools is not the students, classrooms or the system, it is the attitudes and conception of customers themselves. The public still has a distorted view of the schools and blame is placed where blame should not be placed. Therefore, good receptive communications must exist between the school and our customers.

"By the year 2020, the majority of students in America's public schools will be living in circumstances traditionally regarded as placing them at risk of educational failure. Many will be poorly housed, undernourished, subject to the effects of others' abuse of drugs, and provided with few positive adult role models. A greater number of young people will be neglected or abused by those adults who enter their lives and - because of misunderstandings, insufficient resources, or a lack of regard for individual differences and capabilities - treated harshly by the very institutions that ostensibly were created to help them" (Rossi and Stringfield, p. 73).

If these statements prove to be true then by 2020 public dissatisfaction with the public schools will have brought a deterioration of our present school systems. Schools might be desperate to "fix the ills" and not necessarily from inspiration. Privatizations in the school systems could be the result of this panic, desperate stage. If complete take-over by private companies happens there will be less communication between our customers.

For centuries, America has been working hard to improve the education of our children. Reform has been high on every agenda in the nation. As a result, academic standards have been raised, teacher certification requirements have been tightened and educational innovations have been rapid. Contrary to the view of many, progress has been made. The Carnegie Report suggest that American schools are among the best in the nation. However, too many of our schools are still at the marginal level. The world has changed, economics and demographics have changed and our schools have had to change, too. The lives of children who enroll in our schools today will be tomorrow's great leaders. "If, in the days ahead, educators cannot help students to become literate and well informed, if the coming generation cannot be helped to see beyond the confines of their own lives, the nation's prospects for the future will be dangerously diminished" (Boyer, p. 3). The push for school renewal needs a new beginning.

"The creation of new roles and tasks for teachers must be connected to the improvement of teaching as a whole. Such new roles and tasks serve to legitimate teachers' work outside of direct contact with students, would contribute to the creation of a learning community, and would underscore the cardinal professional commitment to continuous growth...The aim of new roles and responsibilities for teachers, however, should not be simply to create a career structure for and retain good teachers. The aim should be to increase the competence of teachers and the effectiveness of schools by bringing the talents of teachers to bear on collective efforts to improve education" (Sykes, 1991, p.).

The Models of Teaching Program in Richmond County, Georgia, provides teachers with on-site training and assistance. The training is conducted by a cadre of specially trained teachers and administrators who assist their colleagues on a variety of instructional methods. They organize faculties into study groups, and incorporate the study of teaching as a part of the regular day. The purpose of the program is to introduce more effective teaching practices and provide a framework for innovation.

For school renewal or a new beginning to take place in the schools, we must first look at the curriculum and teaching methodologies. The curriculum needs to be relevant and more basic skills need to be taught. The curriculum must be integrated so children can make the connections between content areas. The teacher's role should be that of a facilitator and coach. Their methodologies should include teaching to meet individual learning styles in which cooperative learning is part of the teaching style. Cooperative learning enhances a child's skill at being able to work productively as a team member. Alternative student assessments must be included in the evaluation process. Portfolios, peer assessment, checklists and journals are just a few of the many performance based assessments. Ultimately, the hope is to boost student outcomes in terms of academic achievement and the emotional well-being of individuals.

The traditional emphasis on teacher-directed and lecture activities and individual work assignments produce adult employees who are technically competent but lack team skills and problem solving techniques. To prepare students to be successful in the Industrial Age, a greater emphasis must be placed on teaching strategies and learning activities that promote teamwork and leadership. Teacher roles need to change from the autonomous to the collaborative for our present students.

Every student needs to be encouraged to become a disciplined citizen, and a self-motivated learner. The teaching schedule should be flexible and student grouping arrangements need to be varied to promote learning.

In collaborative classrooms, students take an active role in their education by using the teacher as a resource and working with their peers. Examples of collaborative work includes study groups, student projects and research elements. Collaborative education is proven to be successful by both researcher and practitioner. Greater gains in higher order thinking skills and factual knowledge is much greater by using this method of instruction. Cooperative learning develops leadership and group skills, this promotes trust and interpersonal relationships.

The principal plays a vital role in the organization. Tom Peters and Nancy Austin, (1985), state that leadership means vision, cheerleading, enthusiasm, love, trust, passion, obsession, consistency, the use of symbols, paying attention as illustrated by the content of one's calendar, out-and-out drama, creating heroes at all levels, coaching, effectively, wandering around, and numerous other things. Leadership must be present at all levels of the organization.

In other words, a shift in paradigm must occur. Rather than being transactional leaders whose primary functions are managerial, principals are becoming transformational leaders - visionaries, synergists, enablers, and motivators. People who are characterized as Philip Schlechty (1990), "create visions and goals and...cause men and women to transform the institutions of which they are part" (p. 151).

As the leader of the school, the principal is the most visible role model. They have the opportunity and the responsibility to model cultural values and set the standard for staff members. Effective principals are careful to model the values they espouse.

"For years now, studies have been pointing to the pivotal role of the principal in bringing about more effective schools. Our own field studies bear out these findings. In schools where achievement was high and where there was a clear sense of community, we found, invariably, that the principal made the difference" (Boyer, 1983).

Phil Schlechty (1993), stated that a new role for the teacher is an inventor of engaging work. The school board's role is to educate the community about the conditions of schools. And the superintendent's role should be not so much to make decisions as to cause decisions to be made." He further emphasizes that schools are asked to serve a role that we don't fully understand and we're responding to it in terms of the old purpose. "Some schools are organized on the principles of Monopoly while our kids live in an Nintendo world," Schelechty told educators at an ASCD conference. He further elaborated that our students are our customers of work and they must be the focus of all our activities. The school's job is to design activities that meet our customer's needs. We need to make a connection to the real world in the content areas and use these basic skills to solve real life problems. The teacher should be viewed a leader and an inventor. They are to invent work that students will do and to lead them to do it. It's what the teacher does to get the student to do that's important. Formal professional development, in-class support and professional collaboration are likewise critical.

For this change in paradigm to occur in the school renewal, teachers must change. We have experienced limitations of traditional teaching development and only marginal experiencing of the new kinds of learning that are informing the field.

"Reform is not an armchair activity; it is not brought to fruition in state capitals by legislators or state boards of education. It requires energy, commitment, and vision on the part of those who work in our schools" (Bruce L. Wilson and Thomas B. Corcoran, 1987 p.).

Ann Liberman (1995),identified these teacher problems:

- Teachers' professional development has been limited by lack of knowledge about how teachers learn.
- The agenda for reform involves teachers in practices that have not been part of the accepted view of teachers' professional learning.
- Teachers' definitions of the problems of practice have often been ignored.
- Professional development opportunities have often ignored the importance of the context within the teachers' work.

- Strategies for change have often not considered the importance of support mechanisms and the necessity of learning over time.

"If teacher learning takes place within the context of a professional community that is nurtured and developed both within and outside the school, then the effects may be more than just an expanded conception of teacher development. Indeed, such teacher learning can bring about significant and lasting school change" (Lieberman, p. 596).

"The need to change schools seems self-evident. Lectures and textbooks obviously don't motivate students to learn; active student involvement produces more authentic learning. Students should not compete in a win-lose situation; cooperative learning is more productive. Bureaucratic management is incompatible with professionalism; teachers should participate in school governance" (Brandt, 1993, p. 7).

Bill Rauhauser's THE PLANNING BOOK OF EFFECTIVE SCHOOLS (1993), discusses ways to develop a climate which is conducive to learning and for reform to take pace in the classroom. He suggests the following steps:

1. The school climate reflects an atmosphere of trust, respect, high morale, cohesiveness, and caring.
2. There is a student handbook that clearly states expectations for student behavior.
3. A variety of classroom management skills are used to create a businesslike, orderly, and comfortable classroom environment, conducive to learning.
4. Discipline within the school is enforced in a fair and consistent manner.
5. Students come to class prepared.

Why are these innovations and ideals so rare? Many schools lack the funding for staff development and the resources to do them right. Parents and school board members have been resistant in the past, will this be the same story? Staff development and workshops have been generally weak or follow-up has not been conducted to assess progress. Educators sometimes take restructuring in the negative sense, they feel like they are being criticized. We need to overcome these obstacles and get excited about the possibilities of doing things differently.

We need to remember, according to Phil Schlechty, restructuring is merely changing the system of rules, procedures, roles, and relationships that govern the way, time, people, space, knowledge, and technology are used.

Up to this point we've discussed our customers, a mission statement and reform. But, still how do we get one of our customers - the parent - involved in the school? We must invite them and keep inviting them until they come. Realistically, this could be a nuisance but it's worth the pain. Stress to parents that it is our duty as parents and educators to realize that children are our future. In one sense, we are all teachers and should do our part whenever and wherever possible. As a parent, you can help your child succeed in school and in life by helping to teach this lesson: education is important. Just as learning is the key to success, education is the key to learning. As parents we play an important role in determining the habits our children adopt. If we value learning and school, our children will come to value school, too. There are numerous things that parents can do to teach and inspire the love of learning and school. A positive attitude toward education is critical. An appreciation and frequent use of books, magazines and newspapers will set a good example. The effort we make to instill in our children a love for school and learning will result in lifelong enrichment.

Schools can only succeed when parents reinforce the lessons taught at school. The ability to read is one of the basic tools for acquiring knowledge, not only during the early years in school but throughout life. By emphasizing the importance of reading and by conveying to children that learning to read is one of the essential building blocks of success, a parent can play a vital role in a child's success in school and life.

In South Carolina, all schools are required to establish School Improvement Councils to serve as advisory committees to school principals. Comprised of two teachers elected by the faculty, and members of the community, the council's responsibility is to improve the quality of education. During the year, council members collaborate with school staff and administrators to assess school needs, develop and monitor the school improvement plan, and monitor an evaluation process.

The Pearl Public School District in Mississippi seeks parent involvement in education by having a very active P.T.A. at the secondary level. The district formed a Parent Council to keep parents informed about school activities and education related topics. A PEARL PARENT NEWSLETTER is published and distributed to all parents. The newsletter contains information on study skills, school events and positive parenting.

Parents are a child's first role model; therefore, they need to be the best role model possible. Children are so very impressionable and learn to model adults at a very early age.

When parents, teachers and community convey to children high expectations, this will influence children to achieve accordingly. It is evident that when the school, home and community are mutually reinforcing, learning is likely to be the greatest. Bloom states, "The nature of the learning environment is most critical during the periods of rapid change in learning - the early years of school" (1964, p. 68).

Harry Wong (*A Tribute To My Parents* 1991), shares a unique experience with his readers:

" I was five years old and in kindergarten, my parents said something to me over and over again. They even got my relatives to say it to me, as well as my neighbors and the local merchants.

Several times a day, I would hear, "little Harry Wong, when you grow up, what kind of doctor are you going to be? 'This was accompanied by their pointing out to me, as positive role models, that my uncles were all doctors and that my cousins were studying to be doctors.

They told me that it was a foregone conclusion that I would be admitted to medical school, even though the competition was tough in those days. What they wanted to know was what I planned to specialize in.

Not being in kindergarten yet, I said, 'I don't know.'

And then came their reply: 'You're going to be a brain surgeon, aren't you?' In other words, they believed that I had the intelligent to be the ultimate of all doctors.

My parents conveyed a message of high or positive expectations to me. For this I will be forever grateful to them" (p. 41).

We need to convey this important message to each of our children both school, parent and community to be the best you can be regardless of the vocational field a child selects. Have high expectations for children - make them stretch and grow.

Dr. Wong, further states, "The two worst things a parent can give a young person are money and wheels. The two most important things a parent can give a child are roots and wings."

How can we get the community and parents with us in education? How can the schools get indifferent or opposed customers to become a partnership in educating our children? WE need these customers to come inside, we need their expertise. The parent brings expertise - they know the child. They also offer expertise of the customer - our children. We need to say to the parent and the community, we want you here - involved in the school. We also need to tell them, we need your expertise and the valuable data you have about your child. We have to remember these are paying customers and the days of taking them for granted are over. Our schools are in a marketplace competition for support in a world of decreasing resources and increasing demands.

If parents, community and students are not significantly involved in the educational process they cannot and will not support it and in reality they will block our means of improving. They need to understand what is happening. If parents are with you, the communities will also support the effort.

"The more deeply that external group of parents and community is empowered to participate, the greater the power for change it can and will generate. But this is true only if the system views them with respect, sees them as the reason it exists in the first place, and invites their input, their data and their collaboration" (Dolan, 1994, p. 158).

The customer is still fairly a new buzz word to the educational community, we don't yet know the value of our customers. We have to learn how to make the parent and community our customers. This has to be a long-term relationship with dedicated causes outlined in a mission statement. To educate children without this partnership of teacher, parent, community and children is impossible.

Teachers and schools need parent and community support to do their jobs successfully. The education of children is a responsibility shared by teachers, parents, community and children. We need to recognize what a powerful asset a parent and community can be;

what a powerful component these customers are to a school's success. To work effectively, the schools need all customers to support academics, discipline and citizenship efforts.

Shared decision making is a fast growing concept among educators. In 1986 the National Education Association and National Association of Secondary Principals collaborated on VENTURES IN GOOD SCHOOLING, which endorses shared decision making between principals and teachers. Now is the time to extend shared decision making to our other customers - students, parents and community. Our customers need to be involved in the school and its' priorities, long and short rang planning, and school improvement. Support for decentralized decision making is strong among policymakers. In an interview appearing in the NASSP (April, 1991), regarding his membership on the President's Advisory Committee on Education, former Secretary of Labor William E. Brock said, "If you want to unleash American education at its best, give principals and teachers the authority to run their schools, their classes. Miracles will happen" (p.55).

Our schools need to have an inviting climate that goes beyond curriculum and policy and procedures. An effective school provides a climate for learning that is both active and creative not passive for all of our customers. Parents and community must feel welcome and valued in the school setting. They must be made to feel important and a vital part in educating our children. Too many parents and community remember their own experiences in the schoolsetting - these have not always been positive but they have been remembered. Most importantly we need to remember our children and make them the best they can be.

Our school climate also needs to be one of celebration. We need to stand up and celebrate our successes and victories - all customers need to be involved. Not only will recognition improve morale, it also motivates people to reach their highest level of performance.

To enhance staff morale and enthusiasm, the Crawford County Schools in Georgia, offers a PEP WELLNESS PROGRAM, which is a comprehensive wellness program addressing both personal and professional health. This program is designed to help teachers celebrate the successes of teaching.

PROJECT SMILE, in Wake County, Georgia, provides motivation and productivity in a school-based improvement model. They focus on increasing teachers' knowledge base and decreasing teacher isolation.

In their reports on schools recognized as exemplary by the United States Department of Education, cite teacher and principal reward structures among the eight most common characteristics of excellent schools. Varying from Teacher of the Year Programs to honorary titles, these awards provide school personnel acknowledgments of a job well done.

Public celebrations of achievements are often the most motivating forms of recognition. In addition to acknowledging the honoree accomplishments, they glorify organizational values, bond people together, and reinforce commitment. Ceremonies can be small or large, conducted simply or on a large scale - the point is to make a habit of recognizing and celebrating success.

How do we celebrate success for students. In elementary schools success is frequent and given at regular intervals. Award programs are scheduled after each grading period. Students celebrate perfect attendance, academic achievement, most improved in given content areas and many others - the point is - to celebrate. When celebrating remember your other customers - the parents and community - invite them to participate in a child's accomplishments and victories.

The school should be viewed as a place where celebration is part of the schedule beginning the first day of school and taking place throughout the year. At an elementary school in western North Carolina, the first day of school is truly a memorable event. Banners are placed outside and inside the school welcoming students back. The faculty and staff greet each parent and student. An assembly program is held first thing in which students are greeted y the principal and the staff is introduced. Punch and cookies are served in the foyer before the students go to their classes. All staff members have name tags and they are there to serve the valued customers - students and parents. This is truly a memorable occasion for all of our customers.

Another elementary school adopts a vision statement which includes all students will develop reading goals using Accelerated Reader (computerized reading comprehension program). When the vision statement was developed a theme for reading was incorporated and the entire school had a reading "kick-off." Each six weeks students are recognized at awards programs for achieving their reading goals. At the end of the school year a grand finale is scheduled in which students, parents and community have a day filled with celebration.

Obviously, school renewal or reform will have a new beginning. This time the focus seems to be on elementary as the beginning point. However, every level of learning is important and each school level should be emphasized. School failure or displeasure begins early and if all children do not have a good beginning it will be difficult if not impossible to fully compensate and make change at a later day.

What really needs to take place is to have reform movement to the elementary years of the schools, which is by any measure the most important. "We need to go into every classroom, where the teachers meet with students, because that where excellence in education begins and ends. Above all, it's time to stop looking for quick fixes and promising panaceas and begin to put into place the tried-and-true practices that really work" (Boyer, 1995, p. 1). We will continue to hear how the schools have failed, and most definitely, education can improve. "And yet, the longer it goes, the more I've become convinced it's not the school that has failed, it's the partnership that's failed" (Boyer, 1995). Schools are being required to do more and more of the things homes and families are expected to do for their children. The school is becoming the total caregiver. If the schools fail at any given time, they are condemned for not meeting the high expectations. "Yet thirty years of research reveal that it's simply impossible to have an island of educational excellence in a sea of community indifference" (Boyer, 1995). If quality for the schools in America is achieved then parents simply must be actively engaged helping to educate their children. Secretary Riley once said, "The American family is the rock on which a solid education can and must be built."

"I envision a school as a community of leaders, a place whose very mission is to insure that students, parents, teachers, and principals all become school leaders in some ways and at some times" (Barth, 1988).

"As a Nation, we are at a crossroads in deciding not only what we expect from education, but what education can expect from us, individually and collectively. The degree of our commitment will determine whether we graduate to a new era of progress and prosperity or fail our children and ourselves. Like education itself, our decision involves something beyond pragmatism. It is a test of our values" (Clinton, 1996, p. 266).

The Carnegie Foundation surveyed five thousand fifth and eighth graders, thirty-six percent go home each day to an empty house. Sixty percent wanted their parents to spend more time with them. Two thirds wanted more things to do and thirty percent never sat down to a family meal. We are losing sight of our children. "In decisions made every day, we are putting them at the bottom of the agenda.

And while people endlessly criticize the schools, I've concluded that the school is probably the least imperiled institution in our culture. The family is a more imperiled institution" (Boyer, 1995, p. 8). It seems we are focusing on the wrong issues or our priorities are not in order.

The schools are becoming the solutions and the scapegoats to everyone's problems. In many situations, the school is the only stabilizing force that is still working. Schools cannot solve all the social and demographic problems but we do need to stand at a middle ground and build a true partnership with the students, parents and communities. Children are our most precious resource, they are our only resource. We have to commit ourselves to helping this generation of children so another generation can take place. We have to work collaboratively and cooperatively on the best interest of our children.

Ernest Boyer has written an article entitled "Rebuild the Partnership." It says:

From the very first, America has had a love affair with education. Throughout our history the citizens of this country have understood that democracy and formal learning are inextricably interlocked, and the building of a network of public schools has been one of America's most spectacular achievements. In the United States today, 45 million children hurry off each day to 83,000 schools from Bangor, to Mission Bay, California. All this has been accomplished not by a national directive but by local citizens committed to building a network of common schools for the common good.

Education has always been a collaborative endeavor; schools have been successful precisely because they had a network of support. In the early days children often served as apprentices to local craftsman. Neighbors cared for other people's children. In colonial America, teachers were considered teachers of morality, and in most families it was the responsibility of older children to help educate the younger children - a practice that persisted for many generations. Above all, it was parents who were the first and most essential teachers.

But slowly the partnership weakened. Families no longer worked together. Apprenticeships were abolished. Older children became less engaged in the education of younger brothers and sisters. Church and community influence diminished. Neighbors became strangers to one another. And the school, increasingly, became an isolated. disconnected institution, without the essential network of support.

Today, we hear endless talk about how the public schools have failed. And surely education can improve. But it's not necessarily the schools that have failed. Increasingly, schools are being asked to teach only the basics but also to teach decision making regarding drugs, reduce teenage pregnancy, eliminate graffiti and teach good citizenship.

Schools can and do coordinate social services. They are trying to meet the needs of all the social, physical, emotional and intellectual needs of all children. Schools cannot do this alone. The unavoidable truth is we cannot have an island of excellence in a sea of community indifference; if we want better education, we must put back together the partnerships we once had.

We need collaborative efforts among business, industry, colleges and schools, especially projects that give more dignity and more status to teachers and students. If we want better schools, we need parents to turn off the television from time to time and become actively engaged in the education of their children.

John Gardner has written: "A nation is never finished. You can't build it and leave it standing as the pharaohs did the pyramids. It has to be re-created for each new generation." The most urgent task our generation confronts is re-creating public education and rebuilding the partnership between the nation's schools and the communities they serve. (Taken from Dr. Gary M. Fields, Superintendent of Zion-Benton Township High School District 126, Illinois, Conference 1995).

CHAPTER TWO

HOW DO WE PROVIDE A QUALITY EDUCATION FOR OUR CHILDREN?

The quality of public schools is the top issue of concern among American voters reports a new Gallup Poll. While education long has been among the major issues in national politics, this is the first time it has landed as number one.

In the national poll conducted by CNN and USA Today, 76 percent of participating voters said a candidate's position on the quality of the public schools will be a high priority.

This was followed by 66 percent ranking as very high the rate of violent crimes in America, and 66 percent, the nation's economy.

USA Today suggests the rise of public education deserves a spotlight because the economy was the top-ranked voter during the 1992 presidential race and crime was a key factor in the success.

Americans are realizing that we are living in a fast moving world and the fate of our nation is in the hands of our children.

The quality of education is key to the development and continued prosperity of any nation. The United States is in a transition from an industrialized nation to a technological, information-based society. It has become apparent that we need to review and revisit our educational standards and make appropriate changes where necessary to insure that the society in which our children live will be successful.

Futurists agree that a new world is coming our way. The world will have a global economy and a shared destiny which calls for increased productivity. By broadening our vision of quality to include societal payoffs, we can be responsive to our future world.

"A satisfied customer is not enough; a continuously healthy, safe, and well-served customer is better. To achieve this, we must be creative, innovative, practical and open to change. We must add to current models, techniques, and approaches so they can identify and deliver products and services that will be useful in tomorrow's world" (Kaufman and Hirumi, 1992, p. 33).

America must compete in a global economy. International comparisons are only one of several indicators to determine what is taught in our school and how it should be taught. These comparisons can help us evaluate how children will be prepared to contribute to our country's prosperity. American schools must redefine education. Knowledge alone is inadequate; standards need to be developed for all students and they must be relevant.

America must make a critical decision about what it means to be educated. Should we be concerned with having students move up Bloom's Taxonomy to higher and higher levels of knowledge of subject matter, should we be concerned with students' ability to apply knowledge they have acquired?

While European countries tend to teach more applications of skills than American schools, the greatest emphasis on application skills takes place in the Asian countries. In Asia, instruction is based on Bloom's Taxonomy and students move upward with the acquisition of knowledge.

American schools do not seem to hold the concept of preparing students for the world of work. The country seems to believe that preparing students for higher education is both prestigious and more rigorous that preparation for work. Many European countries do not share this same belief, and those which did are reforming the school curriculum to emphasize learning for life and work. In general, preparation for work and higher education should be of equal importance and status. Philosophical differences lead to major differences in educational systems. Most notable is the commitment to a dual educational system. Germany is a good example of this concept. Students in the Federal Republic of Germany, as in other German speaking countries are offered a vocational training on the dual principle. Both training takes place at work and school. Practical, hands-on training is given mainly at work, backed by theoretical training and general education provided in vocational training schools. The average duration of the vocational training is three years.

Choice for parents of schools is also very common in European schools. Greater emphasis is placed on parental choice and stronger local management are increasingly common factors, the ultimate in choice can be found in England in the Great Maintained Schools system which was introduced by the 1988 Education Act. This gives parents the power to take control of their child's school and remove it from Local Authority control. The school is funded directly from central government. Responsibility and accountability for the use of public funds is within the Governing Body, including parent trustees. This concept is similar to America's charter schools, schools of choice or magnet schools.

The diversity of national schools and experiences offer both challenges and opportunities. The increasing mobility of people within our world is already forcing nations to deal with the issue of mutual recognition of qualifications and educational attainment. The real challenge is not the harmonization of existing systems within the world but in the preparation of young people for a world which in many ways we cannot even envisage.

William Daggett, Director of the International Center for Leadership in Education, recently (1995), stated that educational systems serve different purposes for different countries. However, he defined two universal purposes which are, to develop students' intellectual capacity and for them to understand their culture. The American educational system has always been committed to these concepts. In addition, America has always emphasized the need to prepare students to be effective citizens.

After World War II, American high schools, with pressure from parents, began to consider preparing children for higher education as their primary purpose. In the United States education began emphasizing mathematics, science and communication skills in elementary and secondary education for the purpose of advanced study. We have not entertained the notion on how to apply these competencies in the home, the workplace, or society. However, these are areas that are beginning to emerge as Federal funds are being placed more and more in vocational education (programs such as Tech Prep and others have emerged) because our customers are realizing the need to embrace these concepts.

Mark L. Goldstein, TOMORROW'S WORKFORCE TODAY (1995), tells us to forget about restructuring and foreign competition, the biggest issue for the workforce in the 1990's and beyond will be to build and maintain a qualified workforce. He shares the following statistics:

- 12-30 percent of all employees leave their jobs to care for elderly parents.
- Elderly are becoming more dependent on their children.
- Workers are retiring earlier.
- Aging effects not only those aging but job-holding children/
- By 2000, 5-15 million jobs in manufacturing will require new skills.

- 25 percent of 9th graders drop out of school.
- There is a major crisis in education, 80 percent of universities and colleges have to provide remedial courses.
- Women will account for 2/3 of the workforce.
- Through 2000, the labor force will increase at a slower rate since the Depression.

WORK FORCE

1950

Unskilled		60 percent
Skilled		20 percent
Professional Management		20 percent

1987

Unskilled		35 percent
Skilled		35 percent
Professional Management		30 percent

2000 (Projected)

Unskilled		15 percent
Skilled		45 percent
Professional Management		40 percent

Careers in most demand will include: physical therapists, physicians, computer engineering, systems analysts, nursing, radiation technicians, computer operators, clergy, special education teachers, psychologists, and high school science teachers (Editor, MONEY MAGAZINE, ABC - "Good Morning America," December 13, 1995).

"We are entering the greatest transition America has passed through economically, even more difficult than the change from the agricultural era to the industrial era. We are now going from

Industrial America, to Information America, an economy based on information, not raw materials. When you get a transition of this dimension, it affects every single one of our institutions...The entire substructure of life is in upheaval. This era...has started and this is the reason for some of the pain we are going through now" (Futurist Van Wishard, speaking in Asheville, N.C. 1993).

Are our schools preparing our children for the changes that are taking place and the changes in our economy that have already taken place?

While primary responsibility for preparing children remain with the schools, other agencies must also play a role. Most important are the community colleges and the Job Training Partnership Act. As the states provide adult basic education and GED preparation, the community colleges play a critical role in meeting the needs of school dropouts. Serving these recent dropouts has been identified as a critical success factor for the community colleges.

Knowledge, learning, information, and skilled intelligence are the only raw materials of international commerce. If only to keep and improve on the slim competitive edge we will retain in world markets, we must dedicate ourselves to the reform of the education system for all - old and young alike, affluent and poor, majority and minority. Learning is the investment required for success in the 'information age' we are entering.

Parents, students, educators and the community (all customers) must realize the need to restructure our schools. They must also be apprised of the fact that the skills, knowledge and behaviors needed for employment outstrip those needed for entry into higher education. We still need to prepare our children for colleges, universities. Parents and others must recognize that while we continue to prepare our children to be good citizens and ready for higher education - the same techniques will not be useful to this new society of children. We must make learning relevant in our schools and provide them with cooperative work situations. Also, other sources beyond the textbook have to be used. A lot of parents are beginning to complain - my child doesn't bring home a math book each night - the textbook should only be used as a resource and other supplemental materials are to be used to teach and reinforce concepts. Only after parents and community leaders are convinced that schools need to change will we be able to bring about the type of political and community pressure necessary to produce the increased capacity needed for American schools to support moving our schools to more relevant paces of learning.

Imagine a school where each student in every instructional phase was engaged in intellectual exploration. Imagine a school where each teacher in every teaching situation was facilitating and coaching intellectual thought for each student. Imagine a school where each administrator was devoted to removing barriers that blocked student learning and teacher success. This should be America's vision for our public schools. How does this become a reality?

We must begin by redefining our roles of who, what and how we teach. An atmosphere of interchange must be created where problems are identified and explored. We must have a clear understanding of terms, relevant data and a process to direct this action. Schools must again be centers of the community. Technology will be enhanced at each school site. Staff members will constantly be researching, developing and implementing curriculum to insure the intellectual development of all students.

If American schools intend to stay in business and move into the 21st century, changes must occur in the public schools. The focus must be on customer competition and schools of excellence.

The following are standards which must be met:

1. Schools must always strive for excellence and improvement - no status quo.
2. Involve all stakeholders.
3. Students must be actively involved in learning - this customer must participate.
4. The teacher's role needs to be a coach and facilitator.
5. Communications must be frequent with all customers.
6. An equal opportunity must be provided for all customers.
7. Students must be provided functional skills that are necessary to participate in a global world.
8. Schools must focus on the process and not the product.
9. All stakeholders must feel valued and involved in the equational process.
10. Continual assessment must take place.

The structure of schooling must change so that learning becomes the constant and time for learning becomes the variable. The perishability of knowledge dictates that lifelong learning is essential and that schools focus far more on processes and far less on content.

In the opening paragraph of THE THIRD WAVE (1981), Alvin Toffler says, "A new civilization is emerging in our lives, and blind men everywhere are trying to suppress it. This new civilization brings with it new family styles: changed ways of working, loving, and living: a new economy; new political conflicts; and beyond all this an altered consciousness as well. Pieces of this new civilization exist today. Millions are already tuning their lives to the rhythms of tomorrow. Others, terrified of the future, are engaged in a desperate, futile flight into the past and are trying to restore the dying world that gave them birth."

Very often a fresh idea excites the educational world: non-graded schools, authentic assessment, whole language, site-based management, student-directed conferences, cooperative learning and immersion programs. The most recent is Quality Education or Total Quality Management. Will it improve our schools? Is it different? Will it work?

The basic principles of the Quality movement by W. Edward Deming, is a new strategy for educators. Professional magazines, journals and books are loaded with this topic. TQM practices are not as well known or received in the classrooms as in the business world.

W. Edward Deming's name is everywhere, the guru of Total Quality. There is a movement across America which is reforming American education. A new paradigm has been created for education involving TQM principles. The Total Quality Management principles are energizing business, government, social organizations and finally - education.

Deming's work applies to every organization in the world - corporations, universities, service organizations, and schools. He provides a conceptual framework for understanding any system.

Corporations throughout the nation are using the Total Quality Management methods to run their organizations effectively. This has been very successful in the business world and the same principles can be adapted to the classroom and it has the power to make our schools more effective.

TQM is synonymous with Japan's resurrection from World War II. The Japanese claim this could not have happened without Deming and his fellow American statistical experts, Joseph M. Juran and Armand Feigenbaum. Deming and Juran traveled throughout Japan following the war and taught manufacturers how to improve their products by designing quality systems.

At a meeting in Tokoyo in 1956, Deming promised the nation's industrial leaders that if they would adopt Total Quality Management, they would revitalize their markets world-wide within five years. This was virtually unknown in the United States until 1970 and by then Japan had captured the word market.

Now leaders in education are beginning to adopt Deming's principles. Can we recapture the market for education by using these methods of productivity? Will this be our salvation? Yes? No?

Total Quality Management cannot be the only means of the school's success or failure. This method cannot be successful if it's viewed as, "This too shall pass." TQM is not a quick fix and will not be successful overnight. It took the Japanese five years of grueling work and assessment to be successful in the industry world.

Rewards will come to those schools who wait - positive results will emerge when TQM principles become a daily part of the school day. The benefits will become self-evident, people will feel good about themselves and the work environment and they will take pride in what they are doing and their accomplishments. Employees will begin to feel more open and honest and they will take ownership. Productivity will increase and progress will be continual. Opportunities will be provided for professional development and opportunities for personal growth will be evident. Pride and joy will become standard procedures because educators and our other customers will decide the future of our children.

The philosophy of TQM was developed from the business world, it is dedicated to bringing out the best qualities of all of our customers. It is a natural companion with educational leaders in their work to improve our schools.

TQM looks at meeting the needs of customers, including students, teachers, parents, and the public as well as suppliers or all those whose products and services touch schools on a regular basis.

The schools have always sought ideas on how to improve and make education better. TQM offers management support, it requires a systematic approach to the practice of continual improvement and it requires full participation of those who have a stake in education. The system, not individuals, causes result and improvement, which means students, teachers and administrators are not to blame for declining test scores or other assessment results. TQM provides us with the tools for making education better for our children - and that's why schools are in business.

"If it is as some people talk about it. TQM will be nothing more than MBO (Management by Objectives) warmed over unless we change the fundamental paradigm we use to think about schools, If we continue to think about students as products, and test scores as significant measures - as the qualities that we are trying to control - we're just going to beat ourselves to death again. If however, we think about the student as customer for work, and we think about the work itself as the product, and we talk about variance in the quality of the work provided to kids, that's different" (Brandt, 1993, p.10).

Deming's fundamental logic is very simple. It involves three things: understand processes, get control of processes, and improve those processes. You can't control something you don't understand. This is very similar to Convoy's fifth principle, "Seek first to understand."

DEMING'S 14 POINTS

1. Create a constancy of purpose.
2. Adopt a new philosophy.
3. Cease dependence on inspection.
4. Do not award business based on price tag alone.
5. Improve constancy the system of production and service.
6. Institute training.
7. Adopt and institute leadership.
8. Drive out fear.
9. Break barriers among staff members.

10. Eliminate slogans, exhortations, and targets.
11. Eliminate numerical quotes.
12. Remove barriers.
13. Institute a new program of education and self-improvement.
14. Take action to accomplish the transformation.

Education, in the new paradigm will be a process that encourages continual growth and evaluation. It will encourage continual progress through the improvement of student abilities and the expansion of student interests. It will also encourage the growth of one's character. This paradigm will seek to satisfy all customers and they will be involved in the growth process.

The movement to introduce quality management into American schools complements other valuable models for restructuring education. Previous instructional and organizational reforms involved similar beliefs on how children learn. We seek the best for American children which is an ever-improving system that meets and exceeds the learning needs of today's children. Total Quality Management provides the tools and processes to accomplish the mutual aims of all educational reform or restructuring.

Interventions within our current educational system have done very little to accomplish the productivity within our schools. Recent evaluations indicate that the educational improvement strategies advocated by various groups in the 1980's have not resulted in significant improvement. "Some argue that our current system's effectiveness and efficiency has reached its upper limit and, therefore, significant improvements can only be made through a fundamental restructuring of the system" (Branson, 1987). Total Quality management provides a framework for self-reliant students to positively contribute to society and takes quality management beyond customer satisfaction.

Quality is work produced the best it can be, so that everyone understands 100 percent of it. Quality is a pragmatic system of continual improvement. Education is the new paradigm and it will be a process that encourages continual progress through the improvement of one's abilities and the expansion of one's interests. The North Carolina Center For The Advancement Of Teaching developed a Total Quality teaching packet for five educational systems (1996). Included in the package was an anonymous piece from RENEWAL CONNECTION (Spring 1993, Vol.1, No.3), in which Deming's work is correlated to quality schools. They shared the following:

DEMING'S 14 POINTS FOR QUALITY SCHOOLS

1. Quit using fear
2. Upgrade the system of production and service.
3. Adopt a new philosophy.
4. Lead with leadership training.
5. Institute training at all levels.
6. Take action to start the transformation.
7. Yes, to education and training.
8. Start a relationship built on trust and collaboration.
9. Create a constancy of purpose.
10. Halt numerical quotas.
11. Omit barriers between staff areas.
12. Organize together to arrive at slogans, exhortations, and targets.
13. Lift barriers to pride of workmanship.
14. Stop dependence on mass testing.

The 14 Points apply to any profit or non-profit organization. They are interconnected and must be used in combination with the theory of profound knowledge (addressed later).

In 1993, Lincoln County Schools was selected by the North Carolina Business Committee for Education as one of seven districts in the state to pilot the application of Total Quality Management principles to the process of education. TQM has proven to be a successful advantage in many U.S. businesses, contributing to the improved condition of competitiveness and productivity throughout America industry. Lincoln County Schools and its' Total Quality Education partners recognize that education is clearly a very special service. TQE does not conflict with the core values of American education and it does not change the content of instruction. TQE focuses on improving the processes of managing the system and interacting with customers.

Lincoln County Schools are using the basic principles of TQE, which include:

System thinking - A system is a series of functions that work together to benefit the entire organization.

Customer focus - Identify all customers both internally and externally and build the system to meet the customers' needs.

Leadership - A commitment must be made to bring about changes and innovations.

Management by fact - By using measurements and action toward improvement, we can understand how the system works based on data rather than opinion.

Continentals process improvement - Each person must work to make the process better.

Participatory management - All participants must be involved.

Human resource development - The customers involved are the most important asset.

Teamwork - This is the core of TQE.

Long-term commitment - TQE is an evolutionary process and it takes time.

Key strategies include:

Integrate TQE principles into the existing structure. Achieve quick results by involving students. This can be done by focusing on initial training, demonstration and deployment efforts for the classroom teacher.

Use TQE strategies to improve present teaching methodologies. Develop a replica body of knowledge from demonstration classrooms to share internally and externally.

Measure results and compare to past data. Continue to improve using measurement data and feedback as base line information.

Transformation, as Dr. Deming describes it, is the continuous and means fundamental change. Transformation does not mean adapting here, fixing a little there. An individual or an organization must completely change its way of thinking. Education must be redesigned from the ground up, based on theory, and profound knowledge" (Brandt, 1992, p. 29).

More and more educators are finding the natural fit of Total Quality techniques in the educational process. TQM, whether viewed from Deming's 14 points, Juran's Triology, or Kaoru Ishikawa's Thought Revolution, can best be understood by the fundamental premises.

Bonstingl, (1992), describes these premises as the Four Pillars of Total Quality Management:

1. Focus on customers and suppliers, so school programs and procedures are in the best interest of the students and community

that the school serves. The school is responsible for providing long-term educational welfare of students by teaching them how to learn and communicate in quality ways, how to assess their work and how to invest in lifelong learning. The school's secondary stakeholders and customers are the parents, businesses members of the community and taxpayers. The secondary customers have a right to expect progress in students' progress and for them to become successful, productive citizens.

2. Maintain a constant dedication to improvement, personally and collectively. "The Japanese call this ethos kaizen, a society wide covenant of mutual help in the process of getting better and better, day by day (Bonstingl, p. 6). Schools must have the resources, especially time and money, needed for training and communicating with the stakeholders. Schools have to rethink practices that focus on students' strengths rather than their limitations. Deming suggest we eliminate grades in school from elementary to the university level. This will require educators to re-examine the current methods of assessment. Many schools are creating alternative methods of true assessment which include: portfolios, conferences with parent and teacher, and rubric scoring.

3. The organization must be viewed as a system, and the work people do with in the system must be seen as an ongoing process. A systems process approach must be applied so problems can be solved by analyzing data and changing the organization's structure and relationships. Deming and others suggest that 85 percent of all things that go wrong in any organization are directly attributable to how the organization's system processes are established. "Individual teachers and students, then, are less to blame for failure than is the system - the seemingly immutable pattern of expectations, activities, perceptions, resource allocations, power structures, values, and the traditional school in

general" (p. 7). Schools that have adopted the TQM principles are finding ways to maximize everyone's potential. In the new paradigm of education, continual improvement of learning processes will replace the outdated teach and test methodologies. The focus will be on the process and the product will receive less attention.

4. Strong leadership. A strong and dedicated total quality leadership from top management will ensure that teachers and administrators work successfully to achieve success. According to Deming, leaders must create a constancy of purpose for improvement of product and service. Leaders must establish the parameter in which the schools stay in business and provide jobs through research, innovation and continual improvement of our services and goods. School leaders must focus on establishing the procedures in which our students can succeed best and reach their potential. "Total Quality school environments know that improving test scores and assessment symbols is less important than the progress inherent in the learning processes of students, teachers, administrators, and all the school's stakeholders" (Bonsingl, pp. 7-10).

School systems throughout the nation are recreating and rethinking their work processes and their long and short range planning to accommodate the principles of Total Quality Management.

CAN TOTAL QUALITY EDUCATION SAVE OUR SCHOOL AND PRODUCE QUALITY STUDENTS FOR THE 21ST CENTURY?

Deming's (1982) fist point is to create a constancy of purpose for the improvement of product and service. A mission has to be developed. Unless schools have a clear sense of purpose and know where they are headed the direction is senseless. This brings us to fully understand the organizational structure and scheme. The nest step is to make tentative goals and strategies for completing the goals. Goals should be set high enough so the system can be stretched. Goals should be measurable and fit the school mission statement (Techniques are discussed in chapter three). Once the mission statement and goals have been accomplished the customers need to be provided this information and an orientation to this process

Leadership is the force behind the total quality system. Strong leadership must be evident in the classrooms, school site and at the central office. Leadership must reflect quality in every aspect. A commitment to be quality teachers and principals must be evident before we can teach a quality student. For leadership to occur in the classroom, a customer focus must begin - everything that takes place should correlate with the mission and goals. There is a need for the leader to stay focused at all times. Quality leadership is predicated on an understanding of Deming's profound knowledge. One must have a thorough understanding of application of the system, statistical theory, theory of knowledge, and psychology.

One must fully understand the organization of the system and the sub-systems. In education one must understand the relationship of the classroom to the school site as opposed to the school site and the central office as opposed to the state department as opposed to the national level. Realize how each level operates and upon what authority. Deming agrees that 85-95 percent of all problems within the organization occur due to faulty systems and processes.

Therefore, we have to understand that understanding the operation of a system is mandatory.

The use of data is vital to know what action to be used for the process change to take place. You must understand the system of variation and what invalidates the data. To understand how to use statistical tools and to have a clear understanding of children in the classrooms, are necessary for evaluation purposes.

The theory of knowledge is how we know certain things. Therefore, in thinking about education and the classroom, we have to rethink the way each process interacts with others to create a quality classroom and quality school. The theory of knowledge means the leadership has a complete understanding of the impact of change within the system.

Leaders must understand people and their needs. If certain needs are not met then neither students, parents or colleagues will respond in ways that optimize learning for children.

For quality schools to be effective, the role of the teacher must change. They must demonstrate leadership in the process of education and they must have an active role in the decision making process. TQE and site-based management are natural correlates because both directly involve the customer in decision making. The teacher's role in the classroom also must change - they cannot be mere lecturers but must facilitate instruction and serve as a coach to their customer - the student. This will involve a change of attitude toward students, parents, community and peers. Teachers will serve as coaches and facilitators in the learning process. They will remove the causes of failure in the classroom. If a child fails - the teacher has also failed. Fear from students in the classroom will be reduced - this will take place when a partnership is created among student and teacher. A teacher will understand and expand on the variations among students and teach accordingly. Also, teachers must have adequate professional development. Workshops or inservice training must be provided to teachers on cooperative learning, facilitating, true assessment and principles of total quality.

One important facet of quality schools is to involve those closest to the action in the decision making process. School leaders should listen to teachers, curriculum specialists, students and other customers who have first hand knowledge of classroom needs.

Decisions about a process are best met by joint efforts on the part of customers involved. Cooperative and team relationships extend beyond the school to include external suppliers, agencies and other associations.

Win - win strategies can be developed by respecting the goals of all customers and seeking to establish solutions that satisfy the customer needs.

A principle of quality is based on David McGregor's theories of X and Y. Theory X, is viewed as seeing people as lazy, they work because they have to. This outmoded view, managers are controlling and leading. On the other hand, Theory Y, states that people want to be responsible and involved in their work. Theory Y would hold true for students and employees. The task of management is to arrange organizational conditions so people can achieve their own efforts toward the organization.

Students need to have an active role in the learning process. The day of students merely sitting, taking notes and then regurgitating is over. The student's work must be pertinent to the real world and flow from there. Work needs to be correlated with all content areas where students can have choices, design and reflect upon their choices of learning.

The content of the curriculum must be relevant and interesting for the student. The curriculum must be correlated to the surrounding environment and students must engage in research and development and be treated as the worker. Student work should be classified as active rather than passive.

An emphasis on peer teaching, cooperative grouping and team work should be evident in the classroom. In a classroom structured for these learning methodologies, discipline is least likely to be a problem.

Students should have time in the daily schedule to reflect on their learning experiences. This technique has been very successful in journal writing and letting students share their work with other classes and students.

Continual evaluation should take place in the classrooms and schools. The work produced by the students should constantly be evaluated for skills and content. A variety of assessment must be used such as journals, teacher-student developed tests, student projects and demonstrations. Remember this learning process is a direct reflection on the teacher and both the student and the teacher should share the victory or the defeat.

New activities evolving from the old must constantly take place in the classroom. New activities should spiral from the old activities. The students should understand the quest for quality learning is endless.

Schools should be places of celebration (Boyer, 1992), where student victories and teacher accomplishments are celebrated. Most schools do a good job of recognizing student work - this is typically done at awards or assembly programs. What about the children who don't receive model student or best citizen? Do we still celebrate success with them? Our teachers are really neglected - we observe teacher of the year and other specialties - but what only a few receive these awards, what about the other teachers who are also deserving. Both teachers and students must be recognized for their achievement by other audiences. The audience could be a customer either

internally or externally. The audience must affirm that the work is
important and worth doing.

When creating quality schools, the most important change in
perception is to recognize the school - or really the school district -
precisely as a single, connected system, and to manage it as one.
Unfortunately this perception runs counter with the direct
experiences of many customers. Some employees may have a sense
of how their job influences others as they strive to accomplish the
common goals. Yet, the school district is the smaller, most permanent
system of functions, relationships, and roles for meeting the learning
needs of children. As a single system, a school district is made up of
an interconnected set of components, forces and relationships
working together for a common purpose. When managing schools for
quality, the school district is viewed as an organic or human system,
in which all parts are working together and one can compensate for
another one's weakness. They can work together to become
permanently more effective than they are now, and can become a
system capable of continued growth and vitality.

Each employee in a quality managed school knows how his or
her work and role relates to all the others, and how everyone has the
opportunity to work together for the improvement and optimization
of the whole school system.

"Quality cannot be achieved in certain segments of the system,"
explains G. Thomas Houlihan, former superintendent of Johnston
County School District in North Carolina. "Total quality means just
that: quality in every segment of the system. Custodial practices,
teaching techniques, administrative practices, and boardsmanship
must be examined to focus on total quality. No individual or group
can be exempted, as quality depends upon continual improvement of
everyone associated with the district" (A.S.A., p. 9).

Cultural shifts must occur to achieve total quality, they include:

From:	*To:*
Control management	Commitment management
Task focus	Customer focus
Command	Consensus
Individual work	Team work
Punishment	Celebration
One person making decisions	Customers involved
Lectures	Team work
Standardized test	True assessment
Evaluation	Continual assessment

School leaders in Mt. Edgecumbe High School in Sitka, Alaska, have applied the TQM principles to the work of teachers and students in the classroom and to the establishment of a student-operated salmon export business with Japan. The focus was on the involvement of students in their own continual learning. The quality learning cycle defined lifelong learning. To truly understanding the theory of the quality improvement they understood the necessity for continuous learning. Their goal is to become the nation's model learning community within ten years.

In 1988, when Dr. Harry Reynolds became superintendent of Chattanooga Public Schools in Tennessee, his aim was to restructure the district's resources so they would have a profound impact on children He closed 16 schools and refocused on the teaching and learning process by identifying student not adult needs. This dynamic system used a collaborative process that models high expectations for all students and provides access to and preparation for rich curriculum content that extends from early childhood through high school and continues to post-secondary education. The system is proactive and seeks out, supports and serves each learner with a quality educational program. In Haines, Alaska, teachers and school board members are using these principles.

At Crabtree Elementary, in Waynesville, North Carolina, students have applied TQE principles for curriculum selection and choices. Canton Middle School, in Canton, North Carolina, are using TQM principles for staff development and teacher delivery methods. They are using student directed conferences with parents and teachers.

Haywood County Schools in western North Carolina are focusing on TQM as a countywide goal. Each school has a trained team to conduct staff development and in services. Decisions regarding curriculum and practices are conducted by using the tools of TQM such as light voting, Pareto, and affinity diagrams. All customers are represented in the decision making process.

At a conference, MODELS FOR HIGH STANDARDS FOR NORTH CAROLINA SCHOOLS - AN INVITATIONAL CONFERENCE, (1995), David de Mesquits, Principal and Chief Executive at Mid Kent College in England, stated that American schools did not hold the concept of preparing young children for the world of work in high esteem. He further elaborated that our country seemed to believe that preparing young people for higher education was stressed more. Many European countries do not share this belief. In general, preparation for work and higher education were of equal importance in European nations. Schools are an extension to the larger society, therefore, they vary from country to country and nation to nation.

Dr. William T. Crocoll, Superintendent of Chittenden South School District in Vermont, sought to seek educational structures and programs that were relevant to the changing world and used the principles of TQM. Their premises were that the structure of schooling must change so learning becomes the constant and time for learning becomes the variable. He further noted that schools must focus more on processes and far less on content. Students, parents and teachers prepared personal education plans for each learner using a computer program designed for this application. Although instructional support was primary, teachers also utilized technology to update information on students and to facilitate reporting to parents and community. They had access and could research information for their own professional development. The focus was TQM and on each child. The child assumed the responsibility for learning.

Bonstingl (1992) shared the following pitfalls and obstacles schools face when implementing the Total Quality principles:

Total Quality is not a quick fix, it is definitely long term and it has to be practiced daily.

It takes team work and commitment to the process, workers cannot stand alone and carry on as usual. The top leadership must produce the necessary resources and they must show a commitment to the process.

Training is essential for school staff. Trainers should have a solid understanding of both business and schools so the concepts can be merged successfully.

QUALITY FUSION (1994), by Margaret A. Byrnes and Robert A. Coresky, is a total quality management procedure which evolves from the Foxfire educational approach by Eliot Wiggington (1985). The Foxfire educational approach consists of 11 core practices from a 25 year old approach stated in Appalachia. This approach has been modified with Deming's TQM principles.

QUALITY FUSION, uses an educational approach in which the student is worker and actively involved in the learning process as they meet their customers' expectations (parents and teachers). The authors suggest a holistic approach rather than a linear consequence for the following steps:

1. The mission and goals must be very clear.
2. Leadership must be demonstrated by the teacher.
3. All work must be relevant and be the result of the student.
4. Subject matter must be relevant and connect to the real world.
5. The student is the worker and a team member of the research and development department.
6. Peer teaching, small group work and teamwork are emphasized.
7. Students should be allowed aesthetical experiences.
8. Students and teachers should have reflection time.
9. Evaluation of the learning process should be an integral part of the systems operation.
10. New activities should constantly evolve from the old.
11. There must be an audience other than the teacher.

The Newton Connecticut School District became a total quality school system in 1990. They did not adopt someone else's model but selected a combination of Deming's 14 Points and Glasser's approach to quality. They also used Glasser's Control Theory and Reality Therapy for changes in human behavior and the basic needs drive. Their rationale was that all wants come from undeveloped needs. People are internally motivated to meet individual needs. The staff went through intensive training for three years. The first year of implementation was viewed as research based, they participated in several organizations and received assistance and support. Alternative assessment instruments were developed and teams of teachers established performance standards. A set of core beliefs was developed and it was decided that any action taken for school improvement would depend on the core beliefs.

In 1992 Newton Schools, the faulty and staff were thinking differently and were guided by their logic model. Orientation for new teachers has been changed that balanced unique capabilities and support. A new course is taught by the superintendent (12 hours) in which Deming's 14 Points and Glasser's are incorporated. They concluded that total quality does not cost money but a mere prioritizing of core values. They are constantly improving and this has been a paradigm change for professionals. Their priorities for upcoming years include:

- Staying close to the customer - not loosing sight of the needs of parents and students.
- Over coming the past - management problems claim nearly 90 percent of all organizational problems.
- Expand one's understanding and use tools such as Pareto, run charts, and affinity diagrams. These should be common teaching tools reflected in lesson plan books.
- Application of total quality management techniques to problem solving at all levels of the school system.

Newton School District recommends schools that are considering this management technique should develop their own model. TQE tends to be another educational buzzword and many are jumping on board - without the commitment of staff and administrators. Also, this theme has become so popularized in journals and books, thus, diminishing its' significance. It cannot be considered a quick fix and must be viewed as a long-term process with all customers actively engaged.

A school practicing total quality education meets and exceeds (A.S.A. 1992) the learning needs of its customers - students, parents and communities. If students fail to get jobs or to get into good colleges, or are dysfunctional citizens - they did not receive a quality education. John Jay Bonstingl, (1992) elaborates and states that education, in the new paradigm, will not be a system of fragmented information of the curriculum but education will be a process of continual growth and assessment to improve one's abilities and growth. Education should be good for the individual, economy and for society. Total quality management provides a long-term, systematic, transformational view of reform. In Michigan, the Ingham Intermediate School District defines TQM as a philosophy and a set of principles that uses leadership, quantitative methods, systems analysis and collection of data, and empowerment to continuously improve an organization's capability to meet current and future customer needs.

Educators who are practicing quality methods are consciously making an effort to improve the schools, education of children, society and themselves. Some of the widely agreed upon tenets of quality schools include: (A.S.A. 1992)

- Meeting and exceeding the needs of customers
- Continuous improvement.
- Collaboration with other agencies.
- Identifying core beliefs
- Developing a mission and a vision
- Identify common and special causes of variation.
- Working in teams.
- Investment in employee training.
- Belief that people want to do well and will take responsibility when they see a purpose in their work.
- Managing schools as systems.

Quality is a topic in which there is still a lot of questions. Glasser suggest four conditions and four procedures for building a quality organization (1992, p. 18).

Conditions:

1. Quality is always useful and never destructive.
2. Quality is the best that everyone in the organization, working both separately and together, can achieve at any particular time.
3. Quality is continually being improved.
4. Quality always feels good.

Procedures:

1. Education is a continual process.
2. Lead-managing is practiced as taught by Deming, Juran and others.
3. Understanding is stressed and control theory is practiced.
4. All those working in the organization are treated as professionals.

William Glasser (1990) assisted Rees Elementary School in Utah improve their school and asked them to join the Quality School Consortium. During a three year period, the faculty implemented such practices as multiage grouping, experimental and cooperative grouping, thematic study and global awareness.

Teachers were trained for a week during the summer prior to the Quality School concept implementation. The training took place through Glasser's Reality Therapy Institute.

Parent were involved at the beginning of the school year. They were asked what their child needed the most to be successful in school. Self-esteem and self-confidence were the number one priorities parents selected for their children. Parent-teacher conferences were scheduled and parent-teacher teams were created.

A thematic, integrated curriculum was used. Each teacher selected a theme for six-week units. The classes then rotated so each student was exposed to the different themes.

Specific observation tools have been developed to access student work. Students rate their own work and then discuss the ratings with the teacher. However, the Stanford Achievement Test and end-of-grade tests are still used.

Quality is not a permissive school, Rees Elementary has established rules and students develop a plan to deal with their behavior.

After reading Deming, Glasser, Juran and others on Total Quality Management, where do you go? Examples have been previously provided telling of the success taking place in the schools using the total quality concept.

Before implementing the concepts for a quality school it's always helpful to network with schools that have successfully implemented these concepts. Also, talk to the business world and view their assessment on TQM. It's helpful to invite several schools and business organizations to meet with the faculty and staff to discuss TQM and its' relevance. This is a good time to share resources and form a support group.

Only the customer can be the ultimate judge of quality. In creating quality schools, exceeding customer expectations is the motivation behind all actions. The entire school system is customer focused and is seen as a network of customer/supplier relationship.

In quality schools, a customer is someone or something that uses the product . Whenever people are providing goods, information and/or services to somebody, even within the organization, that someone is the customer. At certain times, each person in the school system is a customer - student, parent, community, faculty, staff and administrators - is a customer, a next in line recipient of a product or service from others contributing to the process. At other times, each person acts as a supplier or provider of goods or services to others in the system.

For schools, some customers and suppliers are external to the system, such as taxpayers and contracted services. However, many customers are internal: those in the school system mutually providing and consuming products and services for each other.

Quality schools listen to their customers and understand the purpose of the customer. These schools improve by careful listening to their customers and are aware of the changing needs that emerge.

Central office staff and principals, are customers and suppliers for each other. Principals supply teachers with the legal parameters of a budget, class schedules, and curriculum guides. Teachers, supply principals with student information regarding attendance, grades and parent feedback. Between teachers, students and principal, a mutual and reciprocal customer relationship should exist. Teachers provide the instructional delivery of competency goals and performance indicators. Students work with each other on class projects and provide the teacher with feedback on progress.

Quality schools challenge educators to look at their district as a system of interrelated processes and people - as a customer/supplier relationship. When the outcome of the school is unacceptable, quality techniques does not look for someone to blame - but it studies the system to see how it can be improved.

Quality programs, to be effective, must move beyond the stage of operational improvement and reach down to the base of the school organization. A school has to go beyond mere surface improvement.

Quality management makes people more accountable because all customers are involved in the victories and the defeats - they all had an active voice in the decisions made. Unity is achieved when everyone shares a common mission, animated decision-making strategies that allows each person a stake in the organization. People have to buy into this process of decision making and leadership. The aim is to build trust and autonomy, offering teachers ownership of their decisions - not everyone wants the responsibility that quality approach brings. This trust and buy-in takes time - if quality programs are to be effective good personal relationships skills must be built.

If you are interested in implementing TQM in a school, the desire needs to come from within the school. You must have financial and technical support to train team-members and you need the administrator's support. In the beginning, you also need outside help. If funds are not available, a partnership with a business or corporation might be feasible. It's also helpful to appoint a full-time coordinator who should be a member of the school or advisory council.

We must stay close to our customer and never think we know all there is to know about the needs of students and parents. While accepting the idea of being customer oriented we really don't know how to do it well. Convincing school staffs that quality is not a quick fix also will take work. Staff members have centuries of combined experience with school leaders jumping on board and opting for the latest innovation that will save our schools. To realize that organizational problems are management problems forces school leaders to acknowledge they have a lot to overcome.

Through training and application, we want to expand our understanding and use quality tools such as Pareto charts, light-voting, fishbones and run charts. These tools should be a common tool used in our lesson planning. By training students and all school personnel, in their use, we can convert data into information that will help other students and programs evaluate their progress.

There is a need to apply quality management techniques to management techniques to problem solving at all levels of the school system. This means training a cadre of facilitators to be available through the school district or at each site. It means that continuous improvement must guide us to our mission.

The benefits of using total quality techniques are astronomical. The synergy created engages all students to become actively engaged in their learning and co-partners in education. Teachers can successfully impact the lives and learning of their students by making the connection between world and classroom. A true partnership can be formed by all of our customers - both internally and externally and the supplier and the customer - we have a common element - student outcomes.

The responsibility for improving the classroom in within the teacher and principal's parameter. Leadership must emerge and action must evident. If the mission is the guiding light then this partnership will be a natural element.

Be sure you have a thorough understanding of quality management and are familiar with all the research - be sure you have a data base that is valid and which you can draw accurate conclusions. Then select those elements that compliment your school's mission and goals. Once total quality is implemented, continue to read and develop your knowledge base. If you have a thorough understanding of this concept you can discuss continuous improvement with co-workers, colleagues, students, parents and community.

During the school year encourage students and teachers to engage in leadership roles. Have them collect data for system change and for personal change.

With change as the only constant in today's world, how can we know the way, go the way and show the way? A positive future awaits our children if we give them the skills they need in school. Throughout the world's educational and corporate realms, enormous efforts are underway to cope with changes. The time has come for educators to realize that things change and must be improved for the sake of our children and other customers. Continuous improvement must be a way of life. As educators we have a responsibility to be role models for our children, one which encourages self-discipline and responsibility. We must also act as problem-solvers so our children will imitate our actions.

If we dismember and/or abandon those schools, teachers and students that are succeeding, we will destroy the very system that offers us hope. If we are to improve our American schools we must:

View evaluation of our students and schools correctly and in light of changing demands, technology and learning.

Support those schools and students who are succeeding.

Look for all the reasons some students fail in school and attack the problems in the homes, neighborhoods and communities where they exist.

Continue to support programs that keep violence and the tools of violence out of our schools. We must also support efforts to remove disruptive individuals from the classrooms where students are actively engaged in the learning process.

Support our teachers. The over-whelming majority are well trained, caring, hard-working and dedicated individuals. We must give them credit and renew their efforts.

Be totally involved in our children's education. Being positive, providing support materials, assisting with homework, attending meetings and conferences and assisting the school and community efforts to be the best we can be.

There is so much good in our schools that we cannot allow their destruction. I fear we have a much larger disintegration of our democratic society.

"A decade after the publication of A NATION AT RISK, educators today have the opportunity to combine efforts with each other, with business and government leaders, with all stakeholders in our common future. We must transform A NATION AT RISK into A NATION OF QUALITY, beginning with the creation of Schools of Quality" (Bonstingl, Nov., 1992, p. 9).

CHAPTER THREE

HOW DO YOU GET CHARACTER EDUCATION?
OR
HOW DO YOU CHARACTER EDUCATION?

"To educate a person in mind and not morals is to create a menace to society." Theodore Roosevelt

What's wrong with our children today? Why can't our children be responsible citizens? It's not nostalgia that provokes this longing today; it's an increase in violence and adolescent behavior cooped with the decline in human values and ethics. Teachers put up with shocking levels of aggression and lack of respect. Police are witness to teens using and abusing alcohol and drugs. Many of today's children receive none or very little guidance from their parents. Fewer community members are taking a look at our children and fewer are attempting to guide them. Instead our children learn about values and morals from television, media and peers. Knowing this, what can educators, parents and community do? We need to build a culture and model the behavior we want our children to emulate. "Admittedly, even the most thorough and well-conceived school programs will often not be enough to counteract negative family and societal influences" (Brandt, p. 3). Schools must develop a cooperative partnership with parents and community. We must do everything we can to make sure our children grow up prepared to act in accord with ethical principles - knowing that they will someday deplore the deficiencies of the next generation.

In the very near future, American schools will be changing drastically and so will the public's relationship with them. On the outside schools will be the same wood and brick, the same we've looked at during the last one hundred years. But the changes will occur from within the structure; classrooms will be modernized with technology and high technical teaching devices. Teaching methodologies and methods of presentations will change. Teachers will have to be backed by volunteers from the community, business, industry and the general public. Educational standards will be more demanding and higher standards of accountability will be enforced. The first instances of reconstruction are well under way - public displeasure with the public schools.

In a report entitled, "Putting First Things First": A Public Critique On School Reform, released by a New York City-based Think Tank, surveyed 1,100 Americans who were asked to give their views on public schools and reform. In large measure, the public, regardless of race, demographics or socioeconomic, wanted higher standards and they realized that the role of the school was expanding. The surveyors wanted to be assured that their schools were safe, orderly, and effectively teaching the basics. Until these conditions are met, the focus on school reform are out of kilter. Number six (out of ten) on the priority list was people wanted the schools to teach values with an emphasis on the stature that allows a diverse society to live together peacefully. The public lack of concern about value issues doesn't mean they endorse education that is value neutral or makes no judgments about moral behavior. There is a realm of broadly agreed upon values people expect schools to teach directly and indirectly.

People traditionally yearn for the "good old days" but they want an improved version of the little red schoolhouse. They want learning to be exciting and fun and for teachers to help students become confident and self-assured.

The New York Think Tank also came out with another report "Assignment Incomplete," in which they concluded that the support for public schools was fragile and shallow. The majority of those surveyed saw private schools as being safer, more secure and promoting values.

An estimated 500,000 attacks and robberies occur in the public high schools each month. Each year nearly three million crimes are committed on or near school grounds - 16,000 per day. Approximately 135,000 students carry weapons to school daily; one fifth of all students report carrying a weapon of some sort. Twenty-one percent of all secondary students avoid using the rest rooms out of fear of being harmed. Surveys of school children reveal that their chief school-related concern is disruptive behavior by other students. Teachers are also concerned. Almost a third of public school teachers indicate they have considered leaving the teaching profession (Kilpatrick, 1992, p. 14).

The situation is even worse outside the school gates. Suicides have skyrocketed over 300 percent during the last thirty years. One in every seven teenagers have attempted suicide. Drug, alcohol and sexual activity is widespread.

These behaviors pose a concern. But many teenagers and adolescents do not seem to be concerned - attitudes are becoming major but in the negative sense. These children are accepting their actions and are not viewing the consequences.

Why aren't we teaching children what's right and wrong? The schools are - they are teaching character education. This concept is based on modeling and learning by example. The schools are also attempting to teach sound decision-making practices and moral reasoning.

Schools need to be re-established as places of "serious moral purpose. In such schools, students would, through the curriculum, be introduced to works of the moral imagination. But the reform that is needed goes beyond changing the ethos of the schools themselves. They can no longer afford to be neutral bureaucracies or shopping malls or service providers. They need to embody the kind of character they hope to instill" (Kilpatrick, 1992, p. 224).

Character education can be a key to being a learning community and for gaining public support. Learning to be a good character is the responsibility of parents and then supported by schools. Parents are the children's first moral teacher. Character education is moral values in action. The schools need to address moral knowing, moral feeling, and moral behavior. They need to stress knowing the good habits of the mind, habits of the heart and doing the good. Good character education is based on universal moral values. There is no such thing as a value free school - teaching is value loaded.

Schooling is core activities and it should not require morals being taught; but we don't live in an idealistic world. How many times have we said if parents were doing their job, then the schools could do theirs? Let's get realistic and all stakeholders work together to promote moral, values and character education because one cannot survive without the other. The schools need the parents and communities to help build character in our youth.

One of our biggest responsibilities is to help children develop habits of self-discipline and respect that constitutes character. There are numerous good books on the market. Hillary Clinton's, IT TAKES A VILLAGE offers both personal and national examples of the need for building character in our children. "When it comes to everyday life, however, parents have to concentrate on instilling self-discipline, self-control, and self-respect early on, and then must follow their children to practice those skills the way they would let them exercise their muscles or their brains" (p. 154).

Not all children enter school with parents who set good examples for them. Brian a fourth grade student was brought to the principal's office for calling a little girl, "A f------ b----" and "A f------ w----." When questioned, his reply was, " I was mad and my mom called our neighbor this, if it's all right for her to say then I can too." What are we teaching our children?

People belittle children when they don't know what else to do, this is normally done in anger. The same concept applies to cursing - adults and children curse when they are at a loss for words - it's a compensation for when someone doesn't know what to say and they feel compelled to speak. These habits are normally long formed but easy to get rid of through encouragement and substitution of other words or terms.

When we belittle children sometimes that is what was done to us when we were children and we are merely doing what we have been taught to do. What we are doing by berating and belittling our children is taking away their self-esteem and self-respect. Hillary Clinton defines discipline as teaching (p. 155). Instead of telling children what to do or what not to do - we should be discussing with them the options available and how to make the right choice. Provide opportunities for children to make these discussions and guide them into making the right choice. The goal is self-disciplined children.

We have got to understand the power of positive modeling. We shouldn't worry that our children don't listen to everything we say, we should worry that they do see everything that we do. We need to help our parents and communities understand the power of role modeling. Educators must remember that what we think, do and say has enormous influence on our students.

Schools need to assist with teaching children self-discipline. Several states have passed House Bills and Senate Bills which mandate that educational units teach character development. With the curriculum becoming more crowded and complicated how can they be asked to teach an additional subject? Also, as schools are held more accountable, how is character education measured as it relates to standardized tests? How do we measure character education and how well we have completed this goal? Yes, good character must start at home but what about the homes where children such as Brian live, what do the schools do? Educators must teach and model but it must be a united community effort? How do you go about developing character education?

We must begin by educating ourselves. Learn about character education by reading books, journals and other materials. Learn how character education has helped reduce discipline problems in the school and home, improve academic performance, and prepare young people to be responsible citizens and productive members of society. A good resource list includes:

AMERICAN INSTITUTE FOR EDUCATION DEVELOP-MENT. This is a nonprofit educational research foundation that offers a K-9 education curriculum.

ASCD CHARACTER EDUCATION NETWORK. Sponsored by ASCD and Boston University's Center for the Advancement of Ethics and Character, its mission is to help teachers and administrators struggling with the ethical and character formation aspect of their work.

CENTER FOR THE ADVANCEMENT OF ETHICS AND EDUCATION. Dedicated to helping schools recapture their role as moral educators, the Center has developed a model that emphasizes the curriculum as the primary vehicle for transmitting moral values to the young. The Center publicizes this model primarily through its

"Teacher Academics" for elementary and secondary teachers and administrators. A similar program is directed toward college and university who are responsible for the preparation of future teachers. The Center is also involved in researching and developing curricular materials for use by schools, teachers and parents.

CENTER FOR CHARACTER EDUCATION. An academic alliance of schools and universities bringing together educators interested in implementing a new model for moral education. The Integrated Education Model is based on the view that, a person of mature character, knowledge, affect, and action are integrated.

CENTER FOR THE FOURTH AND FIFTH R's (Respect and Responsibility). Directed by Tom Lickona, this Center sponsors an annual summer institute in character education, published a Fourth and Fifth R's newsletter, and helps form a network of schools committed to teaching respect and responsibility, and related core values as the basis of good education.

THE CHARACTER COUNTS COALITION. A project of the Japanese Institute; represents a national partnership of organizations and individuals involved in the education, training, or care of youth. Joined in a collaborative effort to improve the character of America's young people based on core ethical values, the Six Pillars of Character: Trustworthiness, Respect, Responsibility, Fairness, Caring and Citizenship. Aims to combat violence, dishonesty, and irresponsibility by strengthening the moral character of the next generation.

THE CHARACTER EDUCATION INSTITUTE OF CALIFORNIA UNIVERSITY OF PENNSYLVANIA. A regional institute that provides character education support to school districts, higher education, businesses, and parents; facilitates research; and offers character education courses.

THE CHARACTER EDUCATION PARTNERSHIP. A nonpartisan coalition of organizations and individuals concerned about the moral crisis confronting America's youth and dedicated to developing moral character and civic virtue on our young people as a way of promoting a more compassionate and responsible society.

THE CHILD DEVELOPMENT PROJECT. An effort to take research knowledge and theory about how elementary-age school children learn and develop intellectually, socially, and ethically and translate it into a practical program for classroom and school.

COMMUNITY NETWORK. A coalition of individuals and organizations who have come together to encourage the moral, social and political environment. This national organization sponsors annual conference, produces position papers and published a quarterly journal.

These are but a few of the organizations that are available to assist with building character and character education.

Being good or nice in middle childhood means two things. First, to be good in the classroom means to be well-behaved, hard working, and respectful of authority. Bad or mean children are disobedient, disruptive and lazy. children who upset the teachers are often the same children who are rejected by peers. Children who are hostile and lack self-control often fail to meet teacher standards of good behavior as well as peer standards of friendship.

As a parent, community member or educator, what is the first step in putting character education in the schools?

Join national partnerships and networks to stay in touch with developments in the area and to receive new information on a regular basis.

Write local school officials and ask them how the schools in your community are providing character education, including community service learning.

Identify a group of administrators, teachers and/or community and business leaders who are interested informing a study group to read and discuss materials about effective character education. Ask your local Board of Education to hold a public meeting which would allow citizens to come together to answer the question "Do you believe that character education should be part of the curriculum?" The answer should be a resounding "Yes." The group would then come to a consensus on those concepts that needed to be included.

How do you get a group of 500 citizens to come to a consensus on character education?

Divide the group into smaller groups and allow them to discuss the different concepts. An excellent document to be discussed is the U.S. Constitution. Allow amble time for discussion and then do pareto voting in which each group member would be given ten votes. They may not use all ten votes on one concept and the most votes to be used is four. Tally the votes and the top numbers would be the choices for the group. These concepts are then placed with the other groups and a final pareto vote is taken. This community has now developed the core concepts to be introduced in character education.

A public awareness committee needs to be formed to coordinate community involvement through a public awareness campaign. The campaign slogan could be "Character Education in Central County." Select a mascot such as an animal or character that serves to coordinate character education; this will help promote the campaign for character education.

A curriculum development committee needs to be formed to correlate the character concepts with the Standard Course of Study. Most states have adopted Character Education Courses of Study. However, character education cannot be taught in isolation; it is to be integrated into the daily course or content of study. Also, teachers are the best models and there are always "teachable moments" in every household and in every school.

Staff Development Committees will assist in developing workshops for educators, community and parents that will help implement character education. Lead contact persons in each region should be trained.

Excellent resources might include: DEVELOPING CHARACTER by Phil Fitch Vincent, EDUCATING FOR CHARACTER: HOW OUR SCHOOLS CAN TEACH RESPECT AND RESPONSIBILITY by Thomas Lickona and WHY JOHNNY CAN'T TELL RIGHT FROM WRONG by William Kilpatrick.

Encourage your county or community to develop a mission statement. For example, "Cumberland County acknowledges that its role is to reinforce traditional values and positive character that originate and are fostered in the home. We will, through collaborative community efforts, teach and model fundamentals of good character to include respect, responsibility, and integrity to all students."

Next, define the concepts and make them a reality. Some concepts might include:

CHARACTER EDUCATION - The teaching of traditional civic and moral concepts of altruism, compassion, courage, courtesy, generosity, honesty, industriousness, integrity, loyalty, obedience, punctuality, respect for authority, responsibility, self-discipline, self-respect, and tolerance.

ALTRUISM - The unselfish interest in the welfare of others.

COMPASSION - To have a sympathetic feeling toward others.

COURAGE - The ability to conquer fear or despair.

COURTESY - A favor courteously performed; politeness.

GENEROSITY - Free in giving or sharing.

HONESTY - Free from deception; truthful.

INDUSTRIOUSNESS - Diligent, busy,

INTEGRITY - To have the inner strength to adhere to higher ethical standards.

LOYALTY - Faithful in allegiance especially to a cause or idea.

OBEDIENCE - Submissive to the restraint or command of authority.

PUNCTUALITY - Habitually acting at an appointed time.

RESPECT FOR AUTHORITY - To act with courtesy and self-control to authority.

RESPONSIBILITY - To be dependable and accountable for one's actions.

SELF-DISCIPLINE - To exercise positive self-control.

SELF-RESPECT - To act with courtesy, tolerance, and dignity.

TOLERANCE - The act or practice of tolerating others especially those with different beliefs or practices differing from one's own.

*These character traits were adapted from the NATIONAL SCHOOL BOARDS ASSOCIATION.

Plan with your community and school to develop ideas for the community. These ideas could be generated at a PTA meeting or a civic event. The following are mere suggestions:

Use billboards throughout the community and town to promote any given concept. The schools may decide to promote a concept a month such as:

September – Altruism	October – Compassion
November – Courage	December – Courtesy
January – Generosity	February – Honesty
March – Integrity	April – Loyalty
May – Obedience	June - Respect for authority

A novel twist would be to associate an animal with each trait. A guidance counselor in Western North Carolina adopted the following for the school:

CHARACTER FOCUS OF THE MONTH – Responsibility
ANIMAL THAT REPRESENTS - Beaver

RELATIONSHIP BETWEEN RESPONSIBILITY AND BEAVERS - Beavers are busy workers and working hard is a way to show responsibility.

BEAVER FACTS - The beaver is dark brown, has large webbed feet, and a broad hairless flattened tail. Beavers live along small wooded streams which they often dam to form what is called beaver ponds.

SUGGESTED ACTIVITIES - Students can write questions about beavers, then research the answers. Make a poster entitled "Responsible Acts." Student can make a list of responsible acts as they occur during the school day. Write the name of the student on the poster who performed the responsible act. Make a sign entitled "I am responsible for my day." Encourage students to read the sign each morning upon entering the class.

This information is shared in each classroom and bulletins throughout the school reflect responsibility and the beaver. This concept is integrated in each classroom and a busy beaver responsibility badge is given to a deserving student each day.

Other characters that are focused on for the rest of the school yet as well as the animals that represent each character include:

Month	Character	Animal
December	Caring	Pelican
January	Self-discipline	Wolverine
February	Fairness	Eagle
March	Honesty	Red Squirrel
April	Citizenship	Raccoon
May/June	Courage	Lion

Ask schools to hold breakfast meetings in which they share the character trait of the month and how it is being taught in the integrated curriculum.

Display children's work both at home and school.

Actively promote the community campaign by adding the logo to advertising.

Ask the churches to dedicate a religious service each month to the character concept.

Provide opportunities for parent education programs (an example would be the Breakfast Club previously mentioned).

Ask coaches and athletic directors to promote character in community sports programs.

Establish a hotline for a safe haven for children. Also, provide a hotline in which parents can call to get information on character education - this could be conducted at the local schools in the evenings by volunteers.

Have students prepare public awareness bulletins and service announcements.

Coordinate community service activities.

Conduct media campaigns stressing the importance of character concepts. People really do listen to those thirty or sixty second recordings on the radio especially if their children are conducting them.

Form a study group among members of other organizations that you belong to such as : neighborhood businesses, professional parents, religious, or service organizations - this will assist in building support for character education.

Invite a character education speaker expert to speak to one or more of the organizations that you belong to and lead a discussion.

Write letters to the editor of newspapers and magazines advocating community support for character education.

Most importantly, model the concepts of character education.

Good character must start at home, must be taught, must be modeled, must be a united community effort and will lead to success. The National Parent Teacher Association has taken a very powerful stance on promoting self-esteem for student success. Self-esteem is often noted as being a key factor in determining how successful students are in school. And, many believe that it is the parents responsibility to ensure good self-esteem in their children. But, parents can't teach things they don't know. Parents often want and need help on their skills in nurturing growth and self-esteem. Studies show that adults with high self-esteem develop children who are confident, trusting and motivated.

HOW CAN PARENT TEACHER ASSOCIATIONS HELP?

P.T.A. can offer a resource list of community agencies that sponsor parenting classes. One elementary school has formed a partnership with a community college in which parenting classes are being taught at the school site. A survey was sent to community members asking what skills were needed and what days and hours would be appropriate for the class. There is no charge for this and the school latchkey (after school care) program is used so daycare services can be made available. Thus far, the program has proved to be successful and approximately 23 adults have enrolled. It is hopeful that the program will expand and other courses such as basic skills and technology can be offered.

Hold parent support groups at the workplace or school. These should not turn into "grip" sessions where the schools are getting beat up.

Ask the media coordinator or guidance counselor to establish a special resource section in the library.

Henry Hoffman in EDUCATIONAL LEADERSHIP, January 1994, made the following recommendation for implementing character education:

1. Identify core values from the community
2. Present the strategies to the staff and community.
3. Write the core values into the curriculum (some states have done this step for us)
4. Ask each school to write a behavioral code that reflects the core values.
5. Encourage all stakeholders to acknowledge their role in the development of ethical students.
6. Provide an ongoing character education program.
7. Develop community service programs at all schools.
8. Ask each school to create a caring environment that ensures success of each student.

There's a lot of good resources available on the market and it is readily flooded with character education material.

Phil Vincent's book, DEVELOPING CHARACTER (1995) is a good resource for teachers, parents and communities. He stresses that to develop moral children and students it is necessary to develop in youth the skills needed for effective thinking and reasoning and moral character and good behavior. He purposes to place these items in the schools. "Based on Plato's teachings we should have schools which are dedicated to the development of the intellect as it relates to the ability to think, reason, and therefore respond to moral concerns" (p. 124). The development of character needs to be integrated in the schools but parents and community leaders must meet and plan a program which will benefit our children, community and nation.

Climate is a term used to describe how people feel about their school. It is a combination of beliefs, values, and attitudes shared by students, teachers, administrators, parents, bus drivers, office personnel, custodians, cafeteria workers, and others who play an important role in the life of the school. When a school has a winning climate people feel proud, connected and committed. They support, help, and care for each other. When the climate is right there is a certain joy in coming to school, either to teach or to learn.

Schools must do something to teach character education in the classrooms. To be successful, teachers and administrators need to know that they can get it done and they are not doing it alone. School climate is evident in one elementary school where they proudly display their motto - Every child a winner every day." This is evidenced throughout the school as you meet students with the logo on shirts and warm up suits. Also, each child that was asked could tell you the motto and what it meant.

"The moral education thing bothers me because I feel as if I'm doing it alone. Many parents seem to enjoy their rights - having a child - but no longer seem to want the responsibilities. I get the feeling, who's helping me here?" (Elementary teacher from N.Y., taken from Lickona 1991).

Schools across the country are trying to promote character development. Chapel Hill required students to do 75 hours of community work before graduation. Parents opposed this requirement and took the school system to court. The court upheld the decision and now it's being appealed. Parents said this requirement invaded the privacy right as upheld by the Constitution. Issues included the 13th Amendment and due process. However, legal issues from character education are really no different than other educational issues. Community service in Atlanta, Georgia have been very successful and students are taking pride in giving something back to the community.

Maryland required ninth grade incoming students to be involved in service learning in 1985. Service had been an elective program in high schools but by 1991 only one percent of the student population was involved in service activities. With support from the Governor, members of the State Legislature, and leaders of prominent businesses and industries, Maryland's educational decision makers concluded that the advantage of service learning were too obvious to leave to elective status (Howard, 1993, p. 42). Service experiences may also impact or reinforce commonly accepted values such as a sense of justice, compassion for others, or acceptance of the obligations of citizens.

A.S.C.D. has designed service learning as a major element of character education initiative. Affiliates of the Association are urged to lead by establishing required programs that span all ages, all students, and, as appropriate, the curriculum and the community.

Elementary and secondary school are participating in such programs as: luncheon meetings with the principal to discuss the responsibilities of the school and how those needs can best be met, PREPARE which is a developed program to help children understand prejudice, CHILD DEVELOPMENT PROJECT which is a grant sponsored by Hewlett Foundation and allows schools to develop a core values program and many other programs have been funded by grants and private donors.

Educators who expect families to participate in the children's school life must give the school a role in helping to enrich family life. We need to ask, what will it take to raise a child to adulthood? Some schools attempt to answer this question by creating classroom communities to meet children's needs. To make this practice work we must be prepared to meet the demands of the parents and change the traditional responsibilities of schools and teachers (Cohl, 1996, p.23). These are indications that things are out of control as we plan to enter a new period of change.

The work of Ernest Boyer and the Carnegie Foundation for the Advancement of Teaching, as presented in THE BASIC SCHOOL, A COMMUNITY FOR LEARNING, provides us with a workable vision for our elementary schools. Boyer provides information that covers every aspect of elementary education. Once again character development is added to the school curriculum. Boyer identifies a number of values that everyone - educators, parents and the community agree. Seven core virtues identified are - honesty, respect, responsibility, compassion, self-discipline, and perseverance - are emphasized to guide a school as it promotes excellence in living, as well as in learning.

We are entering an era in which educators are trying to regain confidence from the public sector.

In a national survey (Report of the Carnegie, Foundation for the Advancement of Teaching) of 22,000 public schoolteachers, 90% say lack of parental support is a problem, 89% report abused or neglected children in their classes, and nearly 70% cite sick and undernourished students.

Success of character education depends on forces outside the school - on the degree in which families and communities join schools in a common effort to foster healthy student development.

A national campaign under the leadership of our White House officials should be started to convince parents how important they are to their children. A lot of parents don't realize how their early actions and attitudes will effect their children's character development. Parents need information on how to insure a family is healthy and happy with good self-discipline and respect for authority figures. Parents are involved in the most important work ever - rising a family.

The change in demographics is a true reflection on American households. In our schools today, 70% of the mothers work, 43% qualify for free or reduced lunches and 67% of the children come from dysfunctional families. Also, schools are asked to provide before and after school daycare. Schools are opening their doors at 6:00am and closing at 6:00pm; these are schools that do not have organized sports. Children have long days at the school.

Governmental agencies must aid in a solution to this problem. Governmental assistance could be given to mothers who are willing to stay home and raise their families with a stipulation being to receive funds, one must provide good citizenship practices. This program could be monitored and revenues dispensed accordingly. The funds spent on this project would exceed the money spent on juvenile delinquency.

If it takes a whole village to raise a child then the community must get involved in the character education of children. Such unity does not occur by accident. It occurs only when people are truly united by a common purpose, by something that reaches beyond the formal structures of the workplace. Our villages have changed and have become fragmented. Grandparents and extended families do not live in the same town, county or even state. In most neighborhoods crime has increased by 110% We have become a society of media - in which we are exposed through radio, television, newspapers, computers, compact disks, cellular telephones and other impersonal communication devices. Technology connects us to the village we used to know. "The village can no longer be defined as a place on a map, or a list of people or organizations, but its essence remains the same; it is the network of values and relationships that support and affect our lives" (Clinton, p. 13).

Community support is essential and we can take advantage of the resources available. Community members can serve in "Big Brother" programs where adults serve as role-models and guidance leaders for children. They also spend time with the child and gain their trust and confidence. There are numerous ways for schools to reach out to the community. Involving grandparents (most of these people are retired) and community members is a way of providing children with that extra attention they may need or lack in their home life.

In 1993, the North Carolina Department of Public Education studied ways to improve character and citizenship education in public schools. An interdisciplinary team collected information on this topic. Character and citizenship became increasingly important in the school setting. State Superintendent, Bob Etheridge, stated, "If schools are to succeed in other areas, such as high academics achievement for all, and if they are to establish safe and orderly learning environments, schools must first succeed in the development and refinement of programs that promote positive character traits, personal responsibility, and responsible citizenship."

Many school systems are implementing successful programs in the area of character education. Others are looking for strategies for refining and initiating such programs. Boards of Education, school administrators and teachers are often asked to make decisions about how to design programs that develop character education, responsible behavior and citizenship in students. This is indeed an enormous task and is not taken very lightly.

"A free society cannot survive unless the values upon which it is grounded are fully comprehended and practiced by each succeeding generation" (Benjamin Franklin).

American mothers, both those who stay home and those who work, spend less than thirty minutes on the average, talking to their children. This is not enough time. In 1993, a study was conducted of working parents, two thirds admitted they did not spend enough time with their children. A portion of time spent together between parents and child is watching television. Mothers who do not work spend more time watching television with children than those who did not. For most mothers, time away from the television was spent doing chores.

Our society has changed and our literature is more concerned with material things and the social changes.

At all ages, literature and good books are gaining renewed interest as being a powerful tool for teaching and reinforcing character education. The schools are constantly striving to get children to be reading on grade level; this is a wonderful tool for integrating communications skills, especially reading with character education. When possible outstanding classroom teachers make the connection with reading and building good character development. Quality literature programs provide the foundation for children to learn and appreciate diversity, respect for different cultures, tolerance, a love for reading and citizenship. Schools that focus on reading encourage children to develop a pleasure for reading and sharing of ideas. It is through this sharing of ideas that schools can help children reflect and examine their ideas and the ideas of others.

Good reading instruction allows children to grow personally as well as academically. Literature selections that place emphasis on respect, responsibility, caring, self-discipline, fairness, honesty, citizenship and courage are developing qualities of citizenship. Discussion with children about reading should be encouraged to provide the application of the characters to the lives of children. Many schools are making literature central to character education. Since reading is an essential component of the basic instructional program, this area of the curriculum is a natural place to integrate character and citizenship.

Literature has changed drastically during the last 150 years. Today's literature is superficial and is loaded with quick fixes and entertaining plots. In contrast, "almost all the literature in the first

150 years could be called the CHARACTER ETHIC AS THE
FOUNDATION FOR SUCCESS - things like integrity, humility,
fidelity, temperance, courage, justice, patience, industry, simplicity,
modesty and the golden rule. Benjamin Franklin's autobiography is
representative of that literature. It is basically, the story of one man's
effort to integrate certain principles and habits deep within his
nature" (Covey, 1990, p. 296).

As educators we owe our children the opportunity for being
exposed to great literature. It should not always be student interest
but selected for them. "Our job as educators should be to nurture in
children the desire to read great literature which has character
development as a primary focus" (Vincent, p. 111). Education should
be on building the child and preparing them to function in an adult
world.

Most great literature focuses on issues of great character. The
quality of the literary selections of the Junior Great Books Program
provides numerous opportunities for character education discussion.
Children participate in collaborative searches for the true meaning of
great work. The Junior Great Books Program is K-12 and
sequentially developed. Selections for primary grades are read aloud
by the classroom teacher; folk tales are very popular at this
developmental age. Grades two through twelve are selected by the
student and take place throughout the world. Selections range from
Shakespeare, Dickens and Beatrix Potter. All of the selections have
something to teach in character education and its application.

Any school concerned with literature and character education
should consider the serious role of a good literary library. The
Advisory Council composed of parents, teachers, community and
students would be the starting place. This group could meet to
discuss the character to be taught and the literary source. Almost all
reading adoptions come with a list of such selections. A reading list
should then be compiled per grade level (This of course will need to

match the competency goals and performance indicators of each grade level). Readings should address specific issues but need to be appropriate for the child's reading level.

But what about parents (other than those few serving on an Advisory Council)? Parents are encouraged to read good literature to their children daily. Allow children to discuss the moral or the values contained in a particular story, poem or writing. This would be a good activity to do when eating dinner or driving in a car. This time would be better spent talking than allowing children to watch television. Phil Vincent (1995), states that the love of reading is often fostered on the lap or the bed of a parent. There are two wonderful consequences which occur when parents initiate early reading with a child. The act of reading and sharing brings a parent and child closer together, there is a bonding both physical and emotional. It also lets a child know that reading and sharing of books is a valued activity, that as a family this is important.

America today suffers from unprecedented rates of teenage pregnancy, drugs, crime and suicide. Most of the programs we have used in the past have not been successful. According to William Kilpatrick, schools and parents have abandoned the moral teaching that was once provided. In WHY JOHNNY CAN'T TELL RIGHT FROM WRONG, (1992), Kilpatrick shows how we can remedy these situations by providing our children with stories, models and inspirations they need in order to become productive citizens who are morally sound.

Children of all ages love to be read to and they enjoy reading alone or with a buddy. THE BEST BOOK OF VIRTUES FOR YOUNG PEOPLE, which is edited and a commentary is provided by William J. Bennett, is an excellent source. This book also comes with a guide for additional practice and discussion. Virtue is defined as "conformity to a standard of right, a particular moral excellence and a beneficial quality or power or thing" (Franklin Speller). This book focuses on ten virtues - self-discipline, compassion, responsibility, friendship, work, courage, perseverance, honesty, loyalty and faith. The stories, poems and writings in this book will help individuals recognize character goals and does a good job of showing examples of the traits. Models and standards in the stories are evident throughout the readings. At the beginning of each section the trait is well defined and written in layperson's terms, followed by poems and stories, some which have been around for years. For example, responsibility is introduced by a poem "F. SCOTT FITZGERALD TO HIS DAUGHTER" in which a father tells his daughter what her duties are. Other stories include: FOR WANT OF A HORSESHOE NAIL, KING ALFRED AND THE CAKES, and THE BELL OF ATRI (adapted from James Baldwin). THE CHEST OF BROKEN GLASS, in which responsibilities of parents and children toward each other change with age. The obligation of honoring father and mother does not stop when parents get old. THE MAN WHO TOSSED STONES, is an ancient Middle East tale which warns us against trying to get rid of our own problems by passing them on to others. These are just a few of the writings contained in THE BOOK OF VIRTUES.

If we could spend twenty minutes a day reading and talking to our children about these stories, our children would be prepared to deal with everyday living.

The core problem facing our schools is a moral one. All the other problems derive from it. Even academic reform depends on putting character first.

EDUCATING FOR CHARACTER (THOMAS LICKONA, 1991), devotes a chapter to schools, parents and community and how they can work together. His objective is to provide readers with one of the greatest challenges our society is facing today and that which is touching our children in the schools and in society - values. We need to teach our children respect, responsibility, hard work, compassion, and other values so desperately needed for successful living in our society. Most parents say they want to help the schools in teaching character education and a basic sense of what is wrong and what is right - but this issue can be controversial. What values should be taught? How should they be taught? He provides practical and successful programs for teaching values and character education that are necessary for our children's moral development. An excellent chapter on peer mediation is included and this information can be adapted for home and school. Today there is a widespread, deeply unsettling sense that children are changing - this tells us much about the society we are living.

Poor parenting is one of the major problems why schools now feel compelled to get involved in character education. The average elementary age child spends 30 hours per week viewing television. By 16, the average child will have witnessed 200,000 acts of violence and by 18, approximately 40,000 sexually heightened scenes.

Ninety-eight percent of American homes have at least one television set which is watched each week for an average of twenty-eight hours by children between the ages of two and eleven, and twenty-three hours by teenagers. Children who grow up in lower-income families, with fewer organized activities, watch more television than more affluent peers. Children admit that certain television shows encourage them to engage in sexual activity before they are ready, behave aggressively, and to be disrespectful to adults. Eighty percent of Americans responded to a 1993 Times-Mirror poll said they believed television was harmful to society and especially to children. Where are the parents and why do they continue to allow their children to watch so much television? Children become immune to violence because they have watched so much on television. What most children are seeing on television can't be good for them (Clinton, 1996).

Defenders of television argue that children are subjected to violence in other media concepts - including fairy tales and other literary classics. However, the tradition of storytelling embodied in fairy tales and modern children's literature assists in developing in children a moral education.

A wave of greed and materialism is suffocating us and the world in which we live. Money is our driving force and what we can do with our money drives our society and our youth. Values education is the hottest topic in our society today. Schools cannot be ethical bystanders at a time when we are experiencing such a turbulent society. Rather, schools must do what they can to contribute to the character development of our children.

"I have come to a frightening conclusion that I am the decisive element in the classroom...As a teacher, I possess tremendous power to make a child's life miserable or joyous. I can be a tool of torture or an instrument of inspiration. I can humiliate or humor, hurt or heal. In all situations, it is my response that decides whether a crisis will be escalated or de-escalated, and a child humanized or dehumanized" (Haim Ginott, 1972).

Respect and responsibility - and all the other values in character education - give schools the moral content they should teach in a democracy. But schools need more than a list of values. They need a concept of character and a commitment to developing it in their children.

"The school system cannot make up for a family failure. The total education of our children is a cooperative effort requiring community solidarity. Apathetic parents who foster a permissive home atmosphere create a problem for everyone" (Lickona, 1991, p. 395).

How many times have you heard, well if he's going to drink I'd rather he did it at home. My gosh the child is only a junior in high school and the parent is breaking the law by even allowing him to drink. What message is this sending to today's generation of teenagers?

The long term success of character education depends on forces outside the school - those in which they have no control over. To the extent to which schools, families and communities connect to develop a common effort to meet the needs of children and foster healthy development will determine how this generation of children achieve life's expectations.

There is an alarmingly increase in the incidents of children lacking respect for authority. Teachers and principals when calling parents about a discipline problem are confronted with "He's your problem when he's at school - you deal with him and you take care of it." Obviously there's a break down between home and school and until both stakeholders realize it's a joint effort and both parties must act responsibly then the breakdown will continue. Parents are being more submissive to the needs and whims of their children and are not always taking the assertive role. For example, a parent is called by a teacher because a child stole money from another child, their response might be, "Well, did you see him/her take it, if not, I don't want to hear about it." More and more parents are refusing to give their work telephone numbers because they don't want to be bothered with school problems. However, not all parents fit these scenarios - we do have concerned parents out there and those that are doing a good job with character development but they are a minority.

Society recognizes the role of the family in developing values and ethics for children. Given the concern in today's society, this role has to be enhanced. Education and character education is a shared responsibility among the family, church, school, and the community.

Parents, teachers, coaches, scout leaders, Sunday School teachers, grandparents,....together we can form a unit of support and guidance for each child in our lives (taken from a third grade teacher at Jonathan Valley Elementary School in Waynesville, North Carolina).

Character education when taught in isolation in the schools has no meaning. Character education must be integrated into the total curriculum. Students must be allowed to explore the place of religion in history, literature, art and music if they are to understand the ultimate beliefs and world views that provide the deepest and strongest sources of human meaning for much of humanity.

In the English language arts curriculum, students have many opportunities to build and strengthen citizenship skills. These opportunities begin as students participate as members of a community of learners in cooperative learning, helping circles/conferences, inquiry project groups, and the direct study of examples of character and ethics in literature. The language skills of the curriculum should provide verbal and written communication as an avenue to affirm and support the development of character and American ethics.

The healthful living education program promotes behaviors that contribute to a healthful lifestyle and improved quality of life for all students.

A guidance curriculum goals and objectives especially incorporate respect for humans and attributes of character primarily focus on the affective and cognitive development of students at all grades.

Decision-making reflecting desired ethics, values and character education should not be taught in isolation, but rather considered a vital component of the entire instructional program. Ethical issues and value-laden decision making based upon sound scientific, mathematical and technological knowledge permeates any curriculum guide.

One of the major roles of social studies is to prepare students for their roles as citizens in a democratic society. If students under the democratic process and are informed, responsible, participating citizens, they will adapt to both their public and private lives. There are many approaches to teaching character education. A multi-approach must be taken with the students. Programs for younger children should focus on concepts that are non-controversial and are supported by the entire community. Political and social issues that could be controversial and diverse are better used with older children.

Approaches to character education vary from community to community, county to county and state to state. Some approaches allow students to do simulations in which they are given problems to confront and solve. Others include a "canned curriculum" developed by leading theorists, consisting of posters and stories that illustrate character traits. A popular approach is to select a character word and activity to be taught on a weekly or monthly basis. These lessons are incorporated into the classroom whenever possible.

By integrating character development in the present school curriculum, the school climate will become more conducive to teaching and learning. Successful character education leads to citizenship and thus leads to an improved school climate.

Each school should have a quality approach to character education and pledge to parents and community 100% continuing improvement of the best work in the child's education. Goals should be set for teachers and students in which one determines strategies to achieve those goals and regularly evaluate progress. Every student should be challenged to do the same to motivate, encourage and achieve their best. It's so important, not just for our success, but for the benefit for all of those young eyes watching our every move, to model a life before them that is worth imitating.

Limits and boundaries need to be established for these children to provide a nurturing, secure environment and to develop good, strong characters in them. It takes time and patience that we don't always seem to have. That's where sacrifices come in; but our children are worth it! What causes damage to a child's self-esteem and emotional development is the lack of structured discipline (which can be defined as neglect), or the other extreme (which can be defined as abuse) of verbal or physical outbursts from the adult. Consistent and pre-determined consequences for inappropriate behavior are necessary to raise an emotionally healthy child.

Arguing with a child is frugal. It undermines the adult's authority and the child loses respect. The child learns that if he pushes, cajoles, and argues long enough, the adult will eventually give in. Thus, in time, the child becomes manipulative and controlling. Parental love (or any kind) does not mean giving to children everything they want. It means to love them enough to set limits and stick to it, to take the time to teach character education, to arrange time to be with them and to listen. Love requires a great deal from each of us, precisely everything.

The partnership between home and school is crucial for the expectation of discipline and order which are necessary for learning. First, parents have to quit making excuses for their children when they misbehave. Frequently, when a principal calls a parent about a child's behavior they will get all kinds of excuses such as: "He's been sick," "He didn't sleep well last night," "His father yelled at him,." "He just doesn't like school," or "He never has liked Mrs. Smith, his math teacher." It's surprising how many times these excuses are used.

How do we assert adult authority? First, we make parents support school authority and quit making excuses for their children. School authorities are not always right but they deserve to be given the presumption they are. This goes back to respect for authority and parents modeling good behavior.

Schools need to be very specific when stating the rules and consequences. Students who are habitual disruptive need to be removed so 28 other students can learn. Standards of conduct should be explained and enforced. Lee Canter (Assertive Discipline) recommends sending home the discipline plan, and asking parents to return it signed.

Schools need to send a very specific message to both parents and students - school is a place for learning and they are expected to act and dress accordingly.

Structure needs to be provided for our children. In spite of good intention parents allow their children too many freedoms before they are ready. Too many young people have emerged too early to be responsible citizens who are contributing members to society. Children do respond when they know the limits.

Harry and Tripi Wong, (THE FIRST DAYS OF SCHOOL, 1991) recommend the following when establishing rules:

1. The most successful classes are those where the teacher has a clear idea of what is expected from the students and the students know what the teacher expects from them.
2. Expectations can be stated as rules.
3. Rules are expectations of appropriate student behavior.
4. After thorough deliberation, decide on your rules and write them down or post them.
5. Communicate clearly to your children what you expect as appropriate behavior.
6. It is easier to maintain good behavior than to change inappropriate behavior that has become established.
7. Rules immediately create a work-oriented atmosphere.

8. Rules create a strong expectation about the things that are important to you.

There are basically two types of rules: General rules which reflect overall guiding principles: Respect others Be polite and helpful Care for other members of the school family

Specific rules tell us what to do. Keep hands, feet and objects to self. Be on time. Do not curse or use profanity. Do not argue with adults.

The main problem facing the classroom is not discipline; it is the lack of procedures and routines. Several school systems have established a Code of Conduct in which it very specifically states the consequences of one's actions.

Lee Canter and Katia Petersen recently (1995), published TEACHING STUDENTS TO GET ALONG, which stresses how to help children work cooperatively in a positive environment. They view the world as being a place where tempers grow short and there's less caring and consideration for others. They take these problems and develop strategies to assist children in counteracting the violence seen on television, on the streets, and in their own homes. The book contains lots of ideas and guidance but it's not a quick-fix. Teaching students to get along is not an easy task and cannot be cured overnight. To be truly successful in helping children learn to get along with others and respond to conflict in peaceful ways, one has to believe in the value of teaching children while they are in reading and math groups.

Cooperative grouping or cooperative learning is a buzz word in education today. It has replaced the sitting in straight rows and doing your own work and not sharing with your neighbor premises. Cooperative learning can be a very important tool in teaching character education. According to Lickona (1991, p. 187), the benefits of cooperative learning include:

1. Teaches the value of cooperation.
2. Builds community in the classroom.
3. Teaches basic life skills.
4. Improves academic achievement, self-esteem, and attitude toward school.
5. Offers an alternative to tracking.
6. Has the potential to temper the negative aspects of competition.

Cooperative learning has the potential to make classrooms exciting and productive work places for children. In a fifth grade classroom a young man wrote in his journal, "I've never been allowed to make decisions about what I want to learn and how I want to learn. It's nice being able to work in a team and with other kids besides your friends. I'm learning a lot." Cooperative learning teaches children that they can work together and not alone and this makes this teaching tool very important in real-life skills. Also, team work can successfully be taught by using cooperative learning.

Forces have combined to thrust on the schools - like it or not - the job of socializing our nation's youth. Schools must pick up the job of socializing students in the values of caring, sharing, and helping. Schools cannot stay out of the area of moral and social development. The evidence on this point is extremely clear. If exclusively traditional classroom structures are used, children become more competitive; if cooperative structures are used, children become more cooperative. And if we must choose some type of classroom structure! The only real question is not if, but how, we are going to impact on the social development of our students" (Spencer Kagen, COOPERATIVE LEARNING, 1992).

Cooperative learning is not a new concept to education but it proves itself very useful in this area of teaching character education.

Training needs to be provided for both teachers and students. Teachers should remind students of the value of cooperative learning and the incorporated character traits. "Cooperative learning represents a wonderful methodology to help mold the character of our children" (Vincent, 1995, p. 87).

As long as educators feel that the recall of information as an end in itself is more important than the application and manipulation of information there will be little incentive towards creating a classroom which utilizes cooperative learning as a tool for education as well as a tool for character development (Philip Vincent, 1995).

1987 Harvard University Study of Violence in Schools, reported that 59% of teachers in urban schools and 40% in rural areas said they face swearing and obscene gestures from students.

In a 1988 Gallup Poll, young adults aged 18 to 29 made the following self-indictment: A total of 89% said their generation was more selfish than people their age twenty years ago, and 82% said they were more materialistic.

In one national survey completed by the Josephson Institute of Ethics in 1990, of more than 6,000 college freshmen and sophomores surveyed, 76% admitted to cheating in high school. (statistics cited by Thomas Lickona, EDUCATING FOR CHARACTER, 1991).

"The shortest and surest way to live with honor in the world, is to be in reality what we would appear to be; all human virtues increase and strengthen themselves by the practice and experience of them" (Socrates).

The key is in the hands of the parents. If American schools are to recover their lost quality, if they are to survive as an economic leader, parents and all stakeholders must accept responsibility for the performance of their students both academically and in character. They must offer themselves as volunteers and role models. They must work with local, state and national politicians to raise school budgets and see that funds are administered to promote effective classrooms in the core subjects and character education. Parents must emphasize to their children the importance of a good education and support them during the difficult job of learning.

The 1994 "Educational Scorecard," the National Education Goals Panel concluded the achievement in America's schools was two-fold, one hopeful and the other discouraging. Unfortunately, the public sees more of the discouraging side than the hopeful one.

Results of the 1994 Gallup Poll of the Public Attitudes Toward the Public Schools contend that fewer people are giving public school high scores and more are saying the schools are not passing - they are failing.

As important as the media makes of test scores, they were not among the top three concerns of the public, according to the annual Phi Delta Kappa/Gallup Poll. The United States public ranks fighting, violence and gangs as the top problem facing schools today. Lack of financial support was number three.

Most public teachers and administrators say they have little power to fix these problems. In a report by the United States Department of Education's Office of Research, only 39% of teachers believed they had considerable influence in shaping school discipline policies; 37% said they had the power to change curriculum and only 33% believe they have the influence to determine the content of in-service programs. The study also states that the public believes the most effective way to stop violence in schools is to establish harsher penalties for students who bring weapons to schools. Honesty was the number one character trait the public wants taught in the schools and they would support schools wanting to teach character education. More than half of the respondents oppose giving tax dollars to parents so they can send their children to private schools. However,

54% believe charter schools - tax supported schools given freedom from policies and bureaucracy are a good idea for education.

Despite these concerns, parents are not rushing their children to private schools - YET. As public school enrollment has increased, private school enrollment has decreased.

Some critics of public schools urge greater competition among the schools as a way of returning control from bureaucrats and politicians to parents and teachers. Hillary Clinton is among the supporters, "I find the argument persuasive, and that's why I strongly favor promoting choice among public schools, much as the President's Charter Schools Initiative encourages. I also support letting public schools determine how they can be managed, including them to contract out services to private firms" (p, 263).

We need to be reminded of the National Goals 2000 and especially number eight: Every school will promote partnerships that will increase parental involvement and participation in promoting the social, emotional, and academic growth of children. Children, parents and communities are our customers but yet we rarely ask them what they need in education. Teachers are the binding force in the school but they too are often ignored when decisions are made. The process of meeting children's needs has to involve all stakeholders in public education.

Parents who know their children's teachers and help with homework and teach their kids right from wrong - These parents can make all the difference" (President Bill Clinton State of the Union Address).

What can be done to help parents and teachers become true partners in their children's learning...and make family involvement in education a basic community value? Secretary of Education Richard Riley in an October, 1994 speech at George Washington University, answered this question. He stated that parents and teachers must work together so our schools can work for our children. Partnerships just don't happen, they have to be developed over a period of time. Riley also said, "The American family is the rock on which a solid education can be built. I have seen examples all over the nation where two parent families, single parents, stepparents, grandparents, aunts, and uncles are providing strong family support for their children to learn. If families teach the love of learning, it can make all the difference in the world to children."

Many children come to school ready to learn. They have the advantage because their parents provide them with safety, and love. They have had experiences that have broadened their minds, increased their communication skills and have better self-esteems. Most of these children have participated in some kind of pre-school before they reach the public skills - this is evident because of the social skills they possess. Most likely these children will be successful in the school setting.

Other children come to school ready to learn but they have disadvantages because their homes lack love and safety. Also, they have never interacted with other peers their own age so they are lacking in social and developmental skills. But they are still ready to learn. Most likely these children will not be successful in school. They will not find success easy because we will not expect them to be successful.

All children can learn. But how many of us actually sincerely believe that all children can learn? Do our actions match our philosophy? Every educator needs to answer this question honestly.

"Children are likely to live up to what you believe of them" (Lady Bird Johnson).

We label children (this is not as common as it was five years ago) but we still have our reading groups. We may not call them red birds, blue birds and buzzards but the children know which group they belong. We need to remember regardless of aptitudes all children have several things in common. They all have the ability to be happy and to love. We must provide conditions in our classrooms which are nurturing to children and meet the individual needs of the children. We must provide conditions which are safe and filled with positive feelings in our classrooms. Schools should be places where children are free to expand their minds and stretch their imaginations and where high expectations for student performance are realized. When we tell a child that he or she is expected to perform at a specific level, that expectation tends to become a reality. Children are not red birds, blue birds or buzzards. Children are children; not small adults. Let's be sure that our actions help each child reach for that star and actually grasp it. Children deserve no less.

"We are what we repeatedly do. Excellence then, is not an act, but a habit" (Aristotle).

Will character education make a difference in our homes and schools?

If we compare character education and the National school violence reports - the answer will be no. But educators and parents both realize that this is a problem which is not going to pass and things will continue to get worse if character education is not taught and reinforced. The paradigm has changed and the focus is on developing character in our children. Based upon research from California's Child Development Project (sponsored by Hewlett Foundation), results have been positive. Significant differences were evident in four areas: classroom behavior, playground behavior, social problem-solving skills, and commitment to democratic values. These gains did not decrease the gains for the academic programs. These children scored as well as their comparison schools counterparts on California's standardized measures of school success. Other research is now underway throughout the nation. The research is difficult when conducting longitudinal studies - these studies require keeping data from pre-kindergarten through a child's graduation.

The effort to evaluate the impact of character education is not new. Even in 1920's, Yale University psychologists Hugh Hartshorne and Mark May studied the behavior of 10,000 schoolchildren who were given the opportunity to lie, cheat, or steal. The frequency of behavior occurrences depended on the moral climate created by the classroom teacher.

The 1970's and 1980's indicated a revelation of moral reasoning and higher stages of development and the influence of classroom teachers developing those higher stages of development.

The 1990's continue to evaluate higher order thinking and cooperative learning. Longitudinal studies have been launched but the concept of character education is relatively new to us today.

School projects such as the Child Development project has proved to be relatively successful (cited previously).

Thirty one schools in Los Angeles use the Thomas Jefferson Character Education Curriculum and the results have been positive. There has been a significant decline in discipline problems in these schools.

The D.A.R.E. Program which is now available in most states has been successful as acting as an awareness program. Incidents of children making the choice to say no to drugs and other issues has increased.

The Q.U.E.S.T. program sponsored by the International Lion's Club has had an impact on student and teacher responses for education. This is a comprehensive program for elementary schools which brings together parents, educators and members of the community to teach children life and citizenship skills. The skills are taught in the areas of self-discipline, responsibility, good judgment and getting along with others. The curriculum is designed to reinforce social and academic skills in the areas of language arts, social studies, health and guidance. This program also creates a positive school climate to focus on solving conflicts between students.

Character education programs are most effective when the school communicates with the parents, lets them know what is being taught, and involves them in planning the curriculum. Corona del Mar High School in Newport Beach, California, recently developed "Respect and Responsibility," which is a program hosting Character Education Day. All stakeholders attended this function (students, parents, teachers, administrators, and community members) Parents were informed of this event and were involved in the planning process. An elementary school in North Carolina established a Breakfast Club which meets monthly with parents, teachers and community. Each month the guidance counselor addresses the character of the month and provides a guest speaker. The character and speaker are suggested by the parents and community. Also, a survey was sent to establish a meeting place and date.

Burlington City Schools, in North Carolina was cited the Governor's Program of Excellence Award for their character education project. A diverse group of agencies assisted the city schools to improve school climate and student behavior by refocusing on the basic principles of character and integrating these principles into the curriculum. Changes included positive differences in interactions between and among students and staff members, declines in disciplinary referrals, and increases in acts of community, provide proof that character education is working to help these youths become worthwhile citizens of tomorrow.

"One of the major functions of education is to develop in students the ability to think clearly and consistently - to enable students to think and rethink regarding their ideas and perspectives. The philosophical life is reflective of this quality. No matter what age the person, the habit of thinking as opposed to simply acting on impulse or letting the mind wander as it will during inactive moments is evidence that the person has taken up the philosophical or thinking life. The goal that we have as educators and parents is to insure that our students possess the ability to think and reason, to engage in the philosophical life" (Joe Hester and Philip Vincent, PHILOSOPHY FOR YOUNG THINKERS, 1987).

Our goal in the schools should be to increase effective communications and encourage community involvement for the benefit of all students. Strategies should include:

1. To develop a plan to enable parents to become effective education partners.
2. To implement a plan to keep parents informed about the changes in practice, curriculum, and methods of instruction.
3. To insure parent involvement and implementation of the schools' Improvement Plans.
4. To strengthen existing business and education partnerships and increase the participation of local organizations and agencies.
5. To develop a plan for system-wide public affairs programs.

Vision statements have become very popular both in the business and education worlds. A good vision statement for a school might include:

SUCCESS FOR TODAY through the cooperative involvement of students, parents, educators and the total community;

PREPARATION FOR TOMORROW through academic achievement for gal students and the development of thinking and reasoning skills; and LEARNING FOR A LIFETIME which assures well-informed, productive citizens for the future (adapted from the Haywood County Schools, Waynesville, N.C.).

Schools should work with families to develop graduates who can set priorities and goals, who are self-disciplined, who have self-confidence, who take pride in accomplishment, who have integrity of character. Opportunities should be provided for students to experience the early life successes which form the foundation for productive, responsible citizenship. Schools should expect that graduates will demonstrate respect and tolerance for others and accept responsibility for improving social and environmental conditions in their community, nation and world.

A school system should strive to build a county-wide sense of shared commitment to the students and programs. School personnel should be expected to build and maintain positive, cooperative working relationships among families, schools, county government, employers, institutions of higher education, and the citizenry. High standards, high expectations, and the cooperative commitment of the whole community should provide our children with the facilities, equipment and other resources needed to prepare them for the future.

We are at a stand-still in deciding not only what we expect from education but what education can expect from parents and community members. Do we believe all children deserve an orderly, safe learning environment? Are we willing to set national standards (again) for teachers, students and schools? Are parents ready to become partners with the schools for the benefit of their children? Are community members, those without school age children ready to join this partnership? If we can answer yes to all of these questions then we are ready to be successful in educating children in character education and the academic core curriculum.

"Yet we have created schools in which our children cannot find the American dream, in which our teachers find they have to protect themselves, and from which our parents find themselves completely isolates. This was our doing; it is our to undo....the solution will begin once we put character first in our schools" (Gauld, p. 1993).

If we truly want to transform our educational system, we must reaffirm our belief in the worth and dignity of each individual. We must renew our American commitment to the proposition that all people are created equally. We must resurrect the pioneering, risk-taking, can-do spirit that built America and made it a great nation. We must communicate to our children that they have an important purpose in life and they have true worth. This can only be accomplished if all stakeholders work together to share this vision and to be sure that this vision becomes a reality to this generation and for generations to come. The complete commitment of parents, community and schools to develop the character in our children will reach the deeper spirits of our children.

The core problem facing the schools today is character and moral values. All other problems are derived from these. All attempts at school restructuring or school reform are impossible unless character education is placed at the top of our priority list. If students don't learn to be responsible citizens are morally responsible for their actions, the number of crimes, suicides, sexual activity and suicides will continue to increase. Academic reforms will have to place character education in their curriculum strategies. Students need to develop self-discipline and respect for human nature. These reforms will be very difficult to make but thy will be impossible without character education being added to the curriculum.

If parents really love their children they will join partners with the schools and insure charter education is taught and reinforced at home.

America has not made a commitment to our number one natural resource - our children. The solution does not appear to be possible on a national or even state level. Only when each individual community understands its role will we improve the status of children in our country.

REFERENCES

Aristotle. 1927. Ethica Nichomachea. THE WORKS OF ARISTOTLE, Vol. IX, translated by W.D. Ross. Oxford; Clarendon Press.

Barr, Robert D. 1996. "Who Is This Child?" KAPPAN. January.

Bennett, Kenneth G. and Bennett Daviss. 1994. REDESIGNING EDUCATION. New York: Henry Holt and Company.

Bloom, Benjamin. 1964. STABILITY AND CHANGE IN HUMAN CHARACTERISTICS. New York: Wiley.

Bonstingl, John Jay. 1992. "The Quality Revolution In Education." EDUCATIONAL LEADERSHIP. November.

Bonstingl, John Jay. 1992. "Deming's Fourteen Points Applied to Companies and Schools." privately published. Also, in April, 1992, "Resource Guide for TQM in Texas Schools. Austin, Texas: Texas Association of School Administrators.

Brandt, Ron. 1992. "On Deming and School Quality: A Conversation with Enid Brown." EDUCATIONAL LEADERSHIP. November.

Brandt, Ron. 1993. "How Restructuring Applies To Me." EDUCATIONAL LEADERSHIP. October.

Brandt, Ron. 1993. "On Restructuring Roles and Relationships: A Conversation with Phil Schlehty." October.

Brandt, Ron. 1993. "What Can We Really Do?" EDUCATIONAL LEADERSHIP. November.

Branson, R.K. 1987. "Why Schools Can't Improve: The Upper Limit Hypothesis." JOURNAL OF INSTRUCTIONAL DEVELOPMENT. 15-26.

Byrnes, Margaret A. and Robert A. Cornesky. 1995. QUALITY FUSION TURNING TQM INTO CLASSROOM PRACTICE. Port Orange, Florida: Cornesky and Associates, Incorporated.

Clark, Robert J. 1995. "At A Minimum." THE AMERICAN SCHOOL BOARD JOURNAL. January. 46.

Cohl, Claudia. 1996. "The Future of Education." PRINCIPAL.

_____. "Common Measures." 1994. Phi Delta Kappa. December.

_____.1994. "Putting First Things First A Public Critique On School Reform." New York: Public Agenda.

_____. 1995. "Assignment Incomplete: A Public Critique On School Reform." New York: Public Agenda.

_____. 1992. CREATING QUALITY SCHOOLS. American Association of School Administrators.

Covey, Stephen R. 1989. THE SEVEN HABITS OF HIGHLY EFFECTIVE PEOPLE: POWERFUL LESSONS IN PERSONAL CHANGE. New York: Simon and Schuster.

Curry, Nancy E. and Carl N. Johnson. 1990. BEYOND SELF-ESTEEM DEVELOPING A GENUINE SENSE OF HUMAN VALUE. Washington, D.C.: National Association for the Education of Young Children.

Deming, W. Edwards. 1986. OUT OF THE CRISIS. Cambridge, Mass.: Massachusetts Institute of Technology.

Dolan, W. Patrick. 1994. RESTRUCTURING OUR SCHOOLS. Kansas City, Nebraska: Systems and Organizations.

Ginott, Hiam. 1972. TEACHER AND CHILD: A BOOK FOR PARENTS AND TEACHERS. New York: Macmillan.

Glasser, N. 1992. THE QUALITY SCHOOL TRAINING PROGRAM. Bulletins 1-18. Canoga Park, California: Glasser Institute.

Goldstein, Mark L. TOMORROWS' WORKFORCE TODAY.

Gough, Pauline. B. 1995. "Time For Prescriptions." KAPPAN. September.

Howard, Maurice B. 1993. "Service Learning: Character Education Applied." EDUCATIONAL LEADERSHIP. November.

Kagan, Spencer. 1992. COOPERATIVE LEARNING. San Juan Capistrano, California: Resources for Teachers, Incorporated.

Kaufman, Roger and Atsusi Hirumi. 1992. "Ten Steps to TQM Plus." EDUCATIONAL LEADERSHIP. November.

Kilpatrick, William. 1992. WHY JOHNNY CAN'T TELL RIGHT FROM WRONG. New York: Simon and Schuster.

Lickona, Thomas. 1991. EDUCATING FOR CHARACTER. New York: Bantam Books.

Lieberman, Ann. 1995. "Practices That Support Teacher Development." KAPPAN. April.

Meir, Deorah. 1995. THE POWER OF THEIR IDEAS: LESSONS FOR AMERICA FROM A SMALL SCHOOL IN HARLEM. Boston, Mass.: Beacon Press.

McClanahan, Elaine and Carolyn Wicks. 1993. FUTURE FORCE. California: Griffin Publishing.

North Carolina Parent Teacher Association. I.O.D. Committee. "Self-Esteem for Student Success." N.C. P.T.A. Bulletin. LXXI, Number 4.

Peters, Tom and Nancy Austin. 1985. A PASSION FOR EXCELLENCE.

Pipho, Chris. 1995. "Getting A Return For The Education Dollar." KAPPAN. April.

Rauhauser, Bill. 1993. THE PLANNING BOOK OF EFFECTIVE SCHOOLS. Lewisville, Texas: Rauhauser Publications.

Rossi, Robert J. and Samuel C. Stringfield. 1995. "What We Must Do For Students Placed At Risk." KAPPAN. September.

Stanley, M. Elam and Lowell C. Rose. 1995. "The 27th Phi Delta Kappa Gallup Poll Of the Public Attitudes Toward The Public Schools." KAPPAN. September.

Sweeney, Jim. 1988. TIPS FOR IMPROVING SCHOOL CLIMATE. Virginia: American Association for School Administrators.

Sykes, Gary. 1991. RESTRUCTURING SCHOOLS. Vincent, Philip Fitch. 1995. DEVELOPING CHARACTER. Chapel Hill, North Carolina: New View Publications.

Toffler, Alvin. 1981. THE THIRD WAVE.

Wilson, Bruce and Thomas B. Corcoran. 1987. PLACES WHERE CHILDREN SUCCEED.

Wilson, Kenneth G. and Bennett Daviss. 1994 REDESIGNING EDUCATION. New York: Henry Holt and Company.